THE INTERSECTIONAL OPPRESSION OF DALIT WOMEN IN HIGHER EDUCATION

AYSHA SHAMEER

PREFACE

This book is the culmination of my unwareing dedication to understanding the intersectional oppression of dalit women in higher education.

The foundation of this Work, was a labor of love, driven by an unbridled passion and the dissertation which I done apart of my MA Women studies in university of calicut campus.to amplify the silenced voices of marginalized Communities.

Through my groundbreaking research, I embarked on a transformative journey, bearing witnesses to the experiences of Dalit women in higher education through a qualitative nature of research.Through my research, I sought to uncover the hidden narratives of Dalit women, whose experiences have been silenced and erased for far too long. I listened to their stories, struggles, and triumphs, and I acquired the intersectional barriers faced in higher education and I was transformed by their strength and resilience.

This book is a reflection of my dissertation, expanded and evolved to reach a wider audience. I hope that it will inspire a new generation of scholars, activists, and allies to join the fight against intersectional oppression and to amplify the voices of Dalit women in higher education.By presenting their experiences, this book seeks to foster a deeper understanding of the multifaceted nature of oppression and to inspire meaningful and action toward creating more equitable and inclusive educational environments.

I extend my heartfelt gratitude to all the participants

Aysha shameer

FORWARD

I really fortunate to have found the gem of my life. Mrs Aysha Shameer, I impressed her perspective on this study and her meticulous work for this endeavour. She is such an inspiration for everyone. Her tenacity, hard work and dedication become an irreplaceable asset to her family and Society.

Education aims at dispelling ignorance, attain knowledge and exact dignity of human being. ' Gender equitable education strengthen women's studies and help to improve the lives of women as a social group. The inequalities created by the caste system as one of the most - pressing issue especially Dalit's who experienced worst discrimination it is a social stratification as classification of people and treating as "Lower"

Dalit women are part of marginalised group of people who have been subjected to both physical and mental torture. In the field of higher education, they lack educational guidance, lack of awareness of government scheme etc... Students found various forms of exclusion, physical abuse and as a result higher level of dropouts.

I am sure, this endeavour open readers eyes in regard to the atrocities our world is facing and it gives new perspectives and challenges society's thinking......

Raseena.CM
Asst. prof - Department of English
MES Arts and Science College Pattambi

GRATITUDE

I would like to express my deepest gratitude to everyone who contributed to the completion of this Book.

First and foremost, I would like to thank my Husband SHAMEER.K for the continuous support.his encouragement have been instrumental in shaping the dissertation to turn book

I am thankful to Hod of Department, all the teachers and staff in the Department of Women's Studies University of Calicut. I convey my sincere thanks to my Guide who supported to complete my dissertation work and help rendered by Librarian of the Department Library.

My sincere thanks to my parents and all my friends for their valuable support throughout the journey.

CONTENTS

Foreword

Preface

1. INTRODUCTION 1 - 8

2. DALITH WOMEN AND EDUCATION 9 - 32

3. UNHEARD NARRATIVES OF DALIT WOMEN:" IN THE LENS OF INTERSECTIONALITY" 33 - 43

4. CONSTITUTIONAL SAFEGUARDS 44 - 48

5. SIGINIFICANCE OF STUDY 49 - 52

6. METHODOLOGICAL FRAME WORK OF RESEARCH 53 - 59

7. DATA-DRIVEN INSIGHTS 60 - 77

8. FINDINGS AND SUGGESTIONS 78 - 93

CONCLUSION 94 - 97

BIBILIOGRAPHY 98 – 124

BIOGRAPHY 125 - 126

CHAPTER 1
INTRODUCTION

CHAPTER 1
INTRODUCTION

"Education is the weapon that Dalit women can use to fight against the triple oppression of caste, class, and gender." - Gail Omvedt"

Education in general and higher education in particular is a key tool for India's growth and development, competitiveness and social stability. Education is a fundamental mechanism for social inclusion and is essential to ensure opportunity to participate in the developmental process. In a society where life chances are unevenly distributed, equality of opportunity depends not only on removal of disabilities but also on the creation of abilities (Tawney 1964) especially focusing on education to enhance the capacity. The system of higher education in any society is deeply involved in the creation and dissemination of knowledge as well as developing the skills necessary for its acquisition and utilization among the younger population. Higher education system in India experienced a phenomenal change and is recognized as a powerful instrument for socioeconomic advancement and a vehicle for upward social mobility for deprived and marginalized sections. Higher education in India has witnessed a steep growth trajectory, with India positioning itself as the world's largest higher education system in terms of the number of institutions and second largest in terms of the number of students.

In India, since Independence, education was given prime importance and subsequent governments, initiated efforts to enhance literacy, enrolment in schools, institutes of higher education and technical education. Currently the government spends around 3.8 percent of its GDP on education and about 1.25 percent of its GDP on higher education. It has a total literacy rate of 74.04 percentage compared to the world average of 83.4 percentage (Annual Report 2011-12, MHRD). However, in spite of the significant progress, higher education sector is plagued by several challenges such as inequitable access to higher education for certain caste In India, since Independence, education was given prime importance and subsequent governments, initiated efforts to enhance literacy, enrolment in schools, institutes of higher education and technical education. Currently the government spends around 3.8 percent of its GDP on education and about 1.25 percentage of its GDP on higher education. It has a total literacy rate of 74.04 percentage compared to the world average of 83.4 percentage (Annual Report 2011-12, MHRD). However, in spite of the significant progress, higher education sector is plagued by several challenges such as inequitable access to higher education for certain caste groups, women, rural population and limitations in high-quality teaching and research resulting in sub-optimal outcomes.

The Constitutional framework through the Directive principles of state policy upholds the educational and economic interests of the scheduled castes and tribes with special concern. The positive and protective discrimination and reservations in educational graduation and higher degree programs is still markedly lower than the national average according to UGC report 2011, 15 percentage of the seats are reserved for SC members and 7.5 percentage for ST members and these ratios reflect the corresponding shares of Dalits and Adivasis in the national population. The majority of Indian higher educational institutions are indeed under central- or state-level government control but the number of private institutions has been growing due to the demands from the society as well as market response operating since early 1990's. How and where are the SC/ST students are distributed in private institutions is an area to be explored. It is noted that the southern states have a better profile in terms of female literacy and the trends are continuing in the higher education scenario as well. The enrolment of women in higher education varies from state to state and within a state between urban and rural areas (MHRD, 2011).

Dalit women in India face compounded oppression in higher education due to their intersecting identities of caste and gender. Historically marginalized and ostracized, Dalit women encounter systemic barriers that hinder their educational pursuits and professional advancements. In India, the intersection of caste and gender creates a unique form of oppression for Dalit women, particularly in the realm of higher education. This article explores the multifaceted discrimination faced by Dalit women in higher education institutions, analysing how systemic caste discrimination and entrenched gender biases compound to hinder their academic progress and social mobility. By examining the experiences of Dalit women, this article aims to shed light on the urgent need for intersectional approaches to address these deep-seated issues.

Background and Context

The caste system in India, a deeply ingrained social hierarchy, places Dalits, formerly known as "untouchables," at the bottom. Despite legal protections, caste discrimination persists in various forms, including within educational institutions. Dalit women, situated at the intersection of caste and gender, face dual discrimination that significantly impacts their access to and experience in higher education.

Intersectionality, a term coined by Kimberley Crenshaw, provides a framework for understanding how various forms of oppression intersect and overlap. For Dalit women, intersectionality highlights how caste and gender oppression cannot be examined in isolation but must be understood in their interconnectedness.

Research on Dalit women in higher education reveals persistent barriers. Studies indicate that Dalit women often face hostile environments in educational institutions, including caste-based discrimination from peers and faculty, sexual harassment, and socio-economic challenges. However, existing literature often treats caste and gender as separate issues, failing to fully capture the compounded nature of the oppression experienced by Dalit women. This article seeks to fill this gap by employing an intersectional lens.

Firstly, the deeply entrenched caste system subjects Dalit women to discrimination and exclusion within academic institutions. They often face biases from peers and faculty, which manifest in overt and covert forms of discrimination, from derogatory remarks to unequal opportunities for research and academic collaboration. This pervasive caste bias undermines their confidence and academic performance. Gender adds another layer of oppression. Patriarchal norms dictate that women's primary roles are domestic, discouraging educational aspirations. Dalit women, bearing the dual burden of caste and gender, are often pressured to prioritize household responsibilities over education. Moreover, safety concerns and lack of financial resources further limit their access to higher education. Institutional support systems are also inadequate. Affirmative action policies, though in place, are often insufficiently implemented. The lack of mentorship, scholarship opportunities, and representation in academic leadership positions leaves Dalit women without the necessary support to navigate and succeed in the academic environment.

Despite a strong belief in the importance of education, various socio-economic barriers profoundly impact their academic trajectories. Financial instability is a predominant issue, compelling many to choose professional courses that promise quicker employment opportunities. This financial burden also influences their accommodation choices, with most refraining from selecting hostel facilities to avoid additional expenses.

"In the revered realm of higher education, a stark reality persists, hidden from view like a whispered secret. Dalit women, marginalized by the triple bind of caste, gender, and class, navigate a labyrinthine landscape of oppression, their voices silenced by the weight of centuries-old hierarchies. The hallowed halls of learning, touted as bastions of knowledge and empowerment, instead become a battleground where Dalit women fight for survival, their identities reduced to mere footnotes in the grand narrative of education.

The numbers tell a tale of systemic neglect: a mere 12% of Dalit women enrol in higher education, compared to 35% of their male counterparts. The dropout rates are equally alarming, with 70% of Dalit women abandoning their studies due to financial constraints, discrimination, and societal pressure. The few who brave the odds and secure a seat in the classroom are met with a curriculum that erases their history, their culture, and their experiences.

My analysis and methodology are inspired by an intersectional approach, which is useful in understanding different form of inequality better. An intersectional perspective can explain the social division of gender, race, age, and many others like caste and ethnicity and how these divisions position people differently in a society. Rather than seeing everyone through a homogeneous lens (Collins & Bilge, 2016) .Dalit girls and women fall under the most vulnerable groups in regard to their caste and gender and an intersectional understanding can help in better understanding of their position in the society and the multiple overlapping inequalities they face in terms of their access and experience of education.

This study aims to deepen the knowledge on the barriers and hardship faced by Dalit girls on different levels concerning their access to education and educational experiences. To achieve the objective of the study ,a qualitative research strategy will be adopted.

Yet, it is in these very spaces that the possibility of liberation beckons. By excavating the intersections of caste, gender, and class, we may yet unearth a new paradigm - one that prioritizes the voices, experiences, and perspectives of Dalit women, and paves the way for a more inclusive, equitable, and just higher education system.

This is a story of resilience, of struggle, and of hope. It is a testament to the power of Dalit women's voices, and a call to action for a world that has long marginalized them. In the words of Babasaheb Ambedkar, 'Education is the weapon that can break the shackles of oppression.' Let us wield this weapon, and forge a new path forward - one that is paved with the promise of equality, justice, and freedom for all."

CHAPTER 2

DALIT WOMEN AND EDUCATION

CHAPTER 2

DALIT WOMEN AND EDUCATION

Dalit Women: Navigating the Intersections of Caste and Gender

Dalit women in India occupy a unique and profoundly marginalized position within the country's social hierarchy. As members of the Dalit community, the historically oppressed "untouchable" castes, and as women, they face the compounded burden of caste- and gender-based discrimination (Rege, 1998). This intersectional reality has profoundly shaped their lived experiences, opportunities, and struggles for social, economic, and political empowerment.

Caste, Gender, and the Dalit Women's Burden

The origins of Dalit women's marginalization can be traced back to the entrenched caste system and patriarchal social structures that have long dominated Indian society. Dalits, considered the lowest in the Hindu caste hierarchy, were subjected to severe forms of social, economic, and cultural oppression, including denial of access to education, public spaces, and basic human rights (Guru, 1995). Within this context, Dalit women faced an additional layer of subjugation, as their gender identity rendered them doubly disadvantaged, facing discrimination not only from the upper castes but also within their own communities.

This legacy of oppression has persisted into the contemporary era, with Dalit women continuing to occupy the lowest rung of the social ladder. National data reveals that Dalit women lag behind their upper-caste and male counterparts across a range of socioeconomic indicators, including literacy rates, educational attainment, workforce participation, and access to healthcare (Government of India, 2011). For instance, while the overall female literacy rate in India stands at 65.5%, for Dalit women, it plummets to a mere 54.6% (Government of India, 2011).

Economic Deprivation and Patriarchal Norms

The persistent economic marginalization of Dalit communities is a significant contributor to the educational and social exclusion of Dalit women. Poverty-stricken Dalit households often rely on the labour of their daughters, forcing many Dalit girls to drop out of school and pursue income-generating work to support their families (Thapar-Björkert & Sanghera, 2016). Compounding this economic burden are the pervasive patriarchal norms that prioritize the education of sons over daughters, relegating Dalit women to the domestic sphere and denying them the same opportunities as their male counterparts.

Sexual and Physical Violence

Dalit women's vulnerability is further exacerbated by the alarmingly high rates of sexual and physical violence they face. Deeply rooted in the intersections of caste and gender, these atrocities serve as a means of asserting upper-caste dominance and control over Dalit bodies and communities (National Campaign on Dalit Human Rights, 2006). Dalit women are disproportionately targeted for sexual violence, with some studies estimating that a Dalit woman is raped every 16 minutes in India (National Crime Records Bureau, 2019). The pervasive culture of impunity and the failure of the criminal justice system to address these crimes further compound the trauma and marginalization experienced by Dalit women.

Resilience and Resistance

Despite the immense challenges they face, Dalit women have a rich history of resilience, resistance, and collective action. They have been at the forefront of the Dalit liberation movement, challenging the caste-based and patriarchal structures that have long oppressed them (Rao, 2003). Through the establishment of Dalit women's organizations, they have created spaces for mutual support, political mobilization, and the development of alternative epistemologies that centre their experiences and ways of knowing (Thapar-Björkert & Sanghera, 2016).

Dalit women have also strategically leveraged legal and policy frameworks, such as the Prevention of Atrocities Act and various affirmative action measures, to demand accountability and secure redress for the discrimination and violence they face (Rege, 1998).

Dalit Women and Education

Dalits saw secular education as a key instrument for modernity and emancipation, especially after the end of the nineteenth century. They took education away from the British and Brahman Raj and used it to form their own resistance in colonial India. Dalit Women's Education in Contemporary India is a social and cultural history that examines the social, economic, political, and historical factors that both opened and closed doors for many Dalits, challenging the triumphal narrative of modern secular education. Dalit Women's Education in Modern India is a notable resource for students of history, caste politics, women's and gender studies, education, urban studies, and Asian studies. (Paik, 2014). Dalit women of India have been living in a culture of silence throughout the century. Gail Omvedt a feminist sociologist has called Indian Dalit women "Dalit among Dalit". Dalit women have been experiencing multifaceted discrimination for ages, apparently, Dalit women are triply vulnerable in terms of their gender, caste, and discreet patriarchy from their own community. In the Indian state, caste is an unavoidable factor in education, as it is in many other sectors of public life. Although educational standards have improved throughout the course of Indian history, enslaved Dalits, particularly female children from this caste, continue to experience caste prejudice in society and in the educational system. Despite the introduction of state education plans, the breadth and scope of these measures have not resulted in a greater number of Dalit women enrolling in higher education. Harinath, S. (2014). To get into college, you need a certain amount of money, supplies, and freedom to work. You also need a certain amount of social resources, and information). Contacts, self-assurance, assistance, counsel, etc. Both of these resources are mutually beneficial. They support each other. Differences in access to both economic and social resources. The variations in enrolment in higher education across castes are explained by social capital. Scaria, S. (2014).

There was a widespread attitude in the community that females should not continue their education since they would they would marry and move in with their in-laws. Another major macro-societal barrier was the worry of a girl's reputation and family's honour being harmed as a result of concerns about perceived or genuine 'love relationships with other pupils. There were further hurdles to girls attending schools, such as low educational quality, violent instructors, and male harassment, Bhagavatheeswaran, L., Nair, S., Stone, H., Isac, S., Hiremath, T., Raghavendra, T., ... & Beattie, T. S. (2016). Gender disparity levels in the scheduled groupings. Women in these categories have considerably less access to educational and employment resources than males, according to the findings, Dunn, D. (1993). Education has numerous benefits for an adolescent girl. However, there are several challenges to staying in school for an SC/ ST adolescent girl in these two districts, which need to be addressed. Focusing on adolescent girls, especially in rural Northern Karnataka, where they face a wide variety of issues is crucial to allowing them to reach their full potential, Bhagavatheeswaran, L., Nair, S., Stone, H., Isac, S., Hiremath, T., Raghavendra, T., ... & Beattie, T. S. (2016).

It illustrates that, even at the conceptual level, the educational policy fails to unify these functions, which remain sectoral goals. Gender, caste, class, and geography are also important factors in deciding access to higher education in India's multi-cultural and multi-ethnic culture. Gender is once again the all-encompassing negative dimension that confers cumulative and conflicting disadvantages on women. Finally, educational policies and programs are unable to capture the complex social reality inside a single framework, and hence fail to bridge the policy-practice divide, Chanana, K. (1993). Academic disciplines are not objective; rather, they are GD Goenka University Journal of Perspectives in Social Science and Humanities Research, Vol. 1 (1), December 2022, pp. 11-23 15 cultures, each with its own unique lens through which they see and make sense of the world (as cited by Thomas, 1990: 7). There are still sociocultural issues that need to be addressed in rural areas, such as untouchability and restrictions on access to public spaces. On the other hand, the majority of respondents ranked economic woes as the most significant concern, trailed by educational challenges, Asrani, S., & Kaushik, S. (2011).

In spite of India's significant expenditures on primary education, there are still disparities in the amount of time spent in school by gender and caste, with girls from scheduled castes being at a significant disadvantage. It's possible that if there were more women from SCs groups in state legislatures, this disadvantage might be lessened. Specifically, an SCs woman legislator may retain a strong feeling of solidarity, especially with other SCs girls and women, as a result of the intersecting gender and caste/tribe identities that she carries, and she may support legislative legislation that is beneficial to SCs girls. As a result of this, and for this reason, we anticipate that the likelihood of SC/ST girls completing primary school, progressing through the grades, and doing well may improve if they live in a district with a larger number of SCs women serving in state legislatures. We put this theory to the test by using district-level data from the Indian Election Commission between the years 2000 and 2004, as well as data from the 2004/5 India Human Development Survey and the Indian Census from 2001. The presence of SC/ST women in state legislatures was shown to have a favourable association with SC/ST girls' grade completion and age-appropriate grade advancement. However, this association did not seem to have any effect on SC/ST girls' performance in elementary school. It is possible that the gender and caste discrepancies in primary education completion rates in India may be reduced if more women from SC/ST communities served in state legislatures. Our research confirms that gender inequality remains strong in these communities in North Karnataka and gender roles for girls are socially constructed and maintained in this context. This is amplified in the case of SC/ST girls, given their perceived lower status and worth, Scaria, S. (2014).

Higher Education and Dalit women:

Since 1991, several things in India have undergone transformations. The stance of the government has been the subject of the most significant shift. which is reflected in a reduction of state funding to higher education, the entry of private players, an increase in the individual cost of higher education (i. e. the self-financing of higher education), the entry of foreign institutions, a large number of Indian students who go abroad on a self-financing basis, changes in the academic GD Goenka University Journal of Perspectives in Social Science and Humanities Research, Vol. 1 (1), December 2022, pp. 11-23 16 environment of higher educational institutions, the impact on teachers' conditions, and so on. All of these factors have contributed to everything that has to be looked at from a feminist point of view, Bhagavatheeswaran, L., Nair, S., Stone, H., Isac, S., Hiremath, T., Raghavendra, T., ... & Beattie, T. S. (2016). There are increasing higher education institutions, but their quality is questionable, effectively making islands of excellence amidst the sea of mediocrity. Increased accessibility to low-quality higher education systems has democratized mediocrity. There is an issue with both the quantity and the quality of the work. According to the gross enrolment ratio (GER), only 24. 5 percent of people are enrolled full-time in higher education, according to the gross enrolment ratio (GER). Despite the fact that education policy has an elitist tilt in favour of higher education, the situation of higher education is far worse than the state of elementary and secondary education. There has never been a comprehensive study conducted on the level of education received by college students at the national level. Apparently vulnerable caste-like Dalit women or Scheduled caste are more deprived in terms of enrolment and dropouts and their mobility is also hindered due to expenses of higher education.

Students from socially disadvantaged groups, such as Scheduled Castes, Scheduled Tribes, and Other Backward Castes, as well as women who lack social capital and cultural socially disadvantaged groups' academic performance and learning outcomes, Bhagavatheeswaran, L., Nair, S., Stone, H., Isac, S., Hiremath, T. Raghavendra, T., ... & Beattie, T. S. (2016). Higher education may be a catalyst for the establishment of more equitable societies if progressive and inclusive governmental policies and higher education practices are implemented, Sabharwal, N. S. (2021).

Enrolment, Dropouts, and Degree Completion:

This age group has a very low enrolment rate. At this level, there is a significant gap in digital literacy. At this level, the quality is likewise consistently poor. In addition to this, there is a significant degree of absenteeism. According to Educational Statistics at a Glance (ESAG) 2018, the focus on delivering elementary education has reportedly increased the Gross Enrolment Rate across all socioeconomic and gender groups (GER).

In terms of female involvement up through the secondary level, advancements have been achieved, and the Gross Enrolment Ratio (GER) for girls has surpassed that of males. However, the percentage of girls who enrol in higher education is far lower than the percentage of guys who do so. There is a discernible divide, in terms of enrolment rate at the level of higher education, between different socioeconomic groups. The 71st round of National Survey of Student Outcomes (NSSO) was conducted in 2014 and found that dropout rates for secondary school males were very high. The same can be said about the reasons behind this, which include economic activity, a lack of interest in education, and financial restraints. There is a very low proportion of students who continue their education through the secondary school level and enrol in colleges and universities. According to an overview of educational statistics published in 2018 by Educational Statistics at a Glance (ESAG), the focus on ensuring access to elementary education has At the level of education, children from low-income families are overwhelmingly represented in public schools. Because of this, these children are disproportionately affected by the low quality of government schools, which in turn creates a vicious cycle of illiteracy.

The situation is worse for those who are enrolled in higher levels of school. One of the motivations for the development of the National Medical Commission Bill is the need to put a stop to the outrageous tuition costs that are levied by medical schools.

Caste-Wise Enrolment Amongst Different Age Groups:

In addition, there are significant gender differences in access to higher education. Girls have less access than boys, with a GER of 12. 42 percent for males and 9. 11 percent for females. It is important to note that, although female enrolment rates are often lower than male enrolment rates, Males from lower castes, girls from lower castes, and various religious groups have more difficulties in gaining access to resources. Females with a greater level of education. In 2004-05, for example, compared to the global average of 9. 11 percent, The ST, the SC, and the GER among females were 4. 76 percent, 4. 43 percent, 6. 60 percent, and 19. 53 percent, respectively, for the ST, the SC, and the GER. OBC women, as well as other females. As a result, the ST/SC girls' GER was around five times that of the ST/SC men. In comparison to upper caste ladies, OBC females earn around three times less. University Grants Commission. (2008).

SC and ST children had a higher rate of dropout than children in the OBC and general groups. According to the report, children in rural regions (13. 7

percent) are more likely to drop out of school than children in urban areas (11. 9 percent). The main reasons for dropout given by the families were that "children were not interested in studies, " "cost was too high, " and "children were expected for domestic duties as well as outside jobs to contribute to family income. " When they were married, about 6% of the females dropped out of school. In this research, an effort was made to classify the most common reasons offered by families for their children's dropout. Nearly 46 percent of dropouts were attributed to home circumstances, according to this classification.

School related concerns such as insufficient infrastructure, a shortage of instructors, and other causes contributed to 15 percent of females dropping out and 4% of boys dropping out. It's vital to note that increasing school infrastructure, education quality, and massive investment in school education can only go so far in reducing dropout rates. Unless and until there is a significant increase in family economic position and a shift in societal views, Gouda, S., & Sekher, T. V. (2014).

Education is a cornerstone of individual empowerment and societal progress. For Dalit women in India, however, accessing education is fraught with complex challenges rooted in historical, socio-economic, and cultural barriers. Dalit women, who belong to the lowest strata of the caste system, face a unique intersection of caste-based discrimination and gender bias that significantly impedes their educational opportunities.

The caste system in India, a social stratification that has persisted for centuries, has entrenched Dalits at the bottom of the socio-economic hierarchy. Historically, Dalits were marginalized and excluded from mainstream social and economic activities, including education. This systemic inequity has had a lasting impact on educational access. According to sociologist Gail Omvedt, "The caste system's legacy continues to dictate the socio-economic barriers faced by Dalit communities, restricting their access to quality education" (Omvedt, 1994). The legacy of exclusion and discrimination has resulted in widespread educational disparities that persist to this day.

Challenges and Discrimination Faced by Dalit Women in Higher Education

Dalit women experience a unique form of intersectional oppression where both caste and gender inequalities converge, creating compounded disadvantages. Gender-based discrimination often exacerbates the challenges posed by caste-based discrimination. Scholar Vina Mazumdar notes, "The dual burden of caste and gender discrimination creates a specific educational disadvantage for Dalit women, leading to compounded marginalization" (Mazumdar, 1986). This intersectional perspective highlights how Dalit women face barriers that are more complex than those encountered by men or women from other social strata.

Economic factors play a critical role in shaping educational access. Many Dalit families live in poverty, which significantly impacts their ability to invest in education. Economic historian N. Sukumar observes, "Poverty in Dalit communities translates into diminished educational opportunities, as economic pressures often lead to the prioritization of child labour over schooling" (Sukumar, 2005). Families struggling to make ends meet may prioritize immediate economic needs over long-term educational aspirations, leading to high dropout rates among Dalit girls.

Educational institutions in Dalit-majority areas often suffer from inadequate infrastructure, which further exacerbates educational disparities. Schools in these areas may lack basic facilities, such as adequate classrooms, sanitation, and teaching materials. Educationist K. S. Jain notes, "The lack of basic educational infrastructure in marginalized areas is a significant barrier to the educational advancement of Dalit girls" (Jain, 2007). This deficiency in infrastructure creates an environment where Dalit girls face additional hurdles in pursuing their education, contributing to lower enrolment and higher dropout rates.

The prevalence of caste-based violence and discrimination within educational settings is another significant barrier to educational attainment for Dalit women. Such violence can manifest in various forms, including verbal abuse, social ostracism, and physical violence. Human rights advocate Arundhati Roy emphasizes, "The pervasive nature of caste-based violence within schools often results in a hostile environment for Dalit students, severely impacting their educational experience" (Roy, 2011). This hostile environment not only discourages Dalit girls from attending school but also impacts their overall academic performance and well-being.

In response to these challenges, the Indian government has implemented various policies and programs aimed at improving educational access for Dalit women. These include scholarships, reservations (affirmative action), and free textbooks. However, the effectiveness of these interventions is often inconsistent. Policy analyst Meena P. Rao notes, "The implementation of affirmative action and educational policies for Dalit women is often inconsistent, leading to variable outcomes in terms of access and quality of education" (Rao, 2012). The uneven application of policies and lack of proper monitoring can undermine their intended impact, resulting in varied outcomes across different regions.

Non-governmental organizations (NGOs) play a crucial role in addressing the gaps left by governmental initiatives. Several NGOs are dedicated to improving educational access for Dalit women by providing scholarships, mentorship, and advocacy. These organizations often work directly with marginalized communities, addressing specific needs and challenges. Their efforts can significantly enhance educational outcomes where formal systems fall short. For example, NGOs may provide supplementary educational resources, support for school infrastructure, and advocacy for policy reforms, thereby contributing to improved educational access for Dalit women.

Highlighting success stories of educated Dalit women can serve as a powerful source of inspiration and a tool for changing societal attitudes. Educated Dalit women who have achieved success in various fields can challenge stereotypes and demonstrate the transformative potential of education. Additionally, community support and awareness programs can play a vital role in encouraging educational participation among Dalit girls. By fostering an environment of support and advocacy, communities can help overcome barriers to education and promote greater educational attainment.

Dalit women in India navigate a landscape of education marred by deep-seated inequalities and multifaceted challenges. These challenges are intricately woven into the fabric of historical, socio-economic, and cultural dynamics. The intersection of caste and gender exacerbates their educational hurdles, creating a complex web of discrimination and disadvantage.

Caste-Based Discrimination

Historical Marginalization: The legacy of the caste system, which historically relegated Dalit's Sociologist Gail Omvedt asserts, "The caste system's legacy perpetuates socio-economic barriers that profoundly limit Dalit communities' access to quality education" (Omvedt, 1994). This historical marginalization has entrenched educational disparities, making it a persistent challenge for Dalit women.

Social Ostracism: In educational settings, Dalit students frequently encounter social ostracism. They may be subjected to exclusion and stigmatization, as noted by educational researcher K. S. Jain, who observes, “The social exclusion and derogatory treatment faced by Dalit students create a hostile learning environment that undermines their educational experience” (Jain, 2007). This ostracism not only affects their academic performance but also their psychological well-being.

Violence and Harassment: The prevalence of caste-based violence within schools further complicates the educational experience for Dalit girls. Human rights advocate Arundhati Roy highlights, “The pervasive nature of caste-based violence within schools results in a hostile environment for Dalit students, severely impacting their ability to engage with and benefit from education” (Roy, 2011). Such violence often leads to high dropout rates and educational disengagement.

Gender Discrimination: Early Marriage and Domestic Responsibilities: Gender biases contribute significantly to the educational challenges faced by Dalit women. Early marriage and domestic responsibilities often curtail their educational opportunities. Scholar Vina Mazumdar notes, “The intersection of caste and gender discrimination often relegates Dalit girls to early marriage and domestic duties, thereby truncating their educational prospects” (Mazumdar,

1986). These societal norms prioritize household responsibilities over academic pursuits, perpetuating educational inequalities.

Limited Mobility: Gendered expectations also restrict the mobility of Dalit girls, particularly in rural areas. The limited access to transportation and societal restrictions on girls' movement pose significant barriers to attending school. As socio-economic analyst Meena P. Rao observes, "Gender norms that restrict mobility and access to education reinforce the educational disadvantage experienced by Dalit girls" (Rao, 2012).

Underrepresentation in Higher Education: Dalit women are significantly underrepresented in higher education. This underrepresentation is partly due to socio-cultural biases and financial constraints. Educational researcher Shanta Sinha emphasizes, "The lack of representation of Dalit women in higher education underscores systemic barriers that inhibit their academic and professional advancement" (Sinha, 2010). These barriers prevent many Dalit women from pursuing advanced studies and realizing their full potential.

Socioeconomic Barriers

Poverty and Economic Constraints: Economic hardship is a formidable barrier to educational access. Many Dalit families live in poverty, which limits their ability to afford essential educational resources. Economic historian N. Sukumar notes, "The economic constraints faced by Dalit families often necessitate prioritizing immediate income-generating activities over education, resulting in diminished educational opportunities" (Sukumar, 2005). This economic reality forces many Dalit children, particularly girls, into labour instead of School.

Child Labour: The necessity of supplementary income drives many Dalit children into labour, which detracts from their educational engagement. N. Sukumar further notes, "Child labour, driven by economic necessity, often leads to high dropout rates among Dalit children, impeding their educational progress" (Sukumar, 2005). This economic pressure exacerbates the educational divide, perpetuating cycles of poverty and lack of education.

Lack of Resources: Schools in Dalit-majority areas often suffer from inadequate infrastructure and resources. The scarcity of essential amenities, such as textbooks and functional classrooms, impedes the quality of education. As educational researcher K. S. Jain highlights, "The deficiency in educational resources and infrastructure in marginalized areas hampers the academic progress of Dalit students" (Jain, 2007). This lack of resources creates an environment where educational attainment is compromised.

Institutional Barriers

Inadequate School Facilities: Many schools in Dalit-majority regions lack basic facilities, further compounding educational challenges. The absence of proper infrastructure impacts the learning environment, making it difficult for students to thrive. As N. Sukumar points out, "Inadequate school facilities in marginalized areas often result in subpar educational experiences and contribute to lower student retention rates" (Sukumar, 2005).

Teacher Bias and Discrimination: Discriminatory attitudes among teachers can significantly affect the educational experience of Dalit students. Such biases result in unequal treatment and lower expectations from Dalit students. Educational researcher Shanta Sinha observes, "Teacher bias and discrimination against Dalit students undermine their educational opportunities and hinder their academic success" (Sinha, 2010). These biases can affect students' confidence and academic performance.

Inconsistent Policy Implementation: Government policies aimed at supporting Dalit education are often inconsistently implemented. Bureaucratic inefficiencies and corruption can prevent the effective delivery of benefits. Policy analyst Meena P. Rao highlights, "The inconsistent implementation of affirmative action and educational policies results in variable outcomes, undermining the intended impact of these measures" (Rao, 2012). This inconsistency affects the accessibility and quality of educational support for Dalit women.

Cultural and Social Attitudes

Stereotypes and Stigma: Deep-rooted stereotypes about Dalit communities contribute to educational discrimination. These stereotypes affect how Dalit students are perceived and treated in educational settings. Scholar Vina Mazumdar notes, "The prevalence of caste-based stereotypes perpetuates educational inequalities, reinforcing societal biases against Dalit students" (Mazumdar, 1986). These stereotypes undermine the aspirations and self-esteem of Dalit girls.

Community and Familial Pressure: Cultural norms that devalue girls' education and prioritize early marriage contribute to educational disparities. Families may face societal pressures that discourage investing in their daughters' education. As socio-economic analyst Meena P. Rao observes, "Community and familial pressures often lead to the undervaluing of girls' education, perpetuating cycles of educational disadvantage" (Rao, 2012). These pressures reinforce barriers to educational attainment.

Lack of Role Models: The absence of visible role models from Dalit communities can affect educational aspirations. The scarcity of successful Dalit women in prominent roles can limit motivation and confidence. Educational researcher Shanta Sinha emphasizes, "The lack of visible role models from Dalit communities constrains the aspirations of young Dalit girls and perpetuates educational inequities" (Sinha, 2010). Role models are crucial in inspiring and motivating students to pursue higher education.

Psychological Impact

Trauma and Low Self-Esteem: The constant exposure to discrimination and violence can have severe psychological effects on Dalit girls. Trauma, anxiety, and low self-esteem can impede their educational engagement. Human rights advocate Arundhati Roy highlights, "The psychological impact of continuous discrimination and violence affects Dalit girls' academic performance and overall well-being" (Roy, 2011). Addressing these psychological barriers is essential for improving educational outcomes.

Fear of Repercussions: The fear of facing further discrimination or violence can deter Dalit girls from pursuing education. This fear often results in irregular attendance and lower educational attainment. As educational researcher K. S. Jain observes, "Fear of repercussions due to caste-based discrimination can significantly impact the educational engagement of Dalit girls, leading to high dropout rates" (Jain, 2007). Creating a safe and supportive educational environment is crucial for overcoming this fear.

The educational challenges faced by Dalit women are deeply entrenched in a web of caste-based discrimination, gender biases, socio-economic constraints, and institutional barriers. Addressing these challenges requires a multifaceted approach that includes improving infrastructure, implementing effective policies, combating social stigma, and providing targeted support. By comprehensively tackling these issues, it is possible to create a more equitable educational environment that empowers Dalit women to overcome historical injustices and achieve their full potential. The educational landscape for Dalit women in India is shaped by a complex interplay of systemic inequities, socio-economic challenges, and institutional barriers. While significant obstacles remain, education offers a powerful pathway to empowerment and social change. Addressing these challenges requires a multifaceted approach that includes improving infrastructure, strengthening policy implementation, supporting non-governmental initiatives, and fostering community engagement. By tackling these issues comprehensively, it is possible to create a more equitable educational environment that enables Dalit women to overcome historical injustices and achieve their full potential.

CHAPTER 3

UNHEARD NARRATIVES OF

DALIT WOMEN:”

IN THE LENS OF

INTERSECTIONALITY”

CHAPTER 3

UNHEARD NARRATIVES OF DALIT WOMEN:"IN THE LENS OF INTERSECTIONALITY"

In the complex landscape of higher education, the experiences of Dalit women stand as a poignant illustration of intersectionality—a term coined by Kimberlé Crenshaw in 1989 to describe how various social identities (such as race, gender, class, and caste) overlap and intersect to create unique modes of discrimination and privilege. In the context of India, the caste system continues to shape societal structures, resulting in systemic disadvantages for Dalits, particularly women.

Understanding Intersectionality

Intersectionality emphasizes that individuals do not experience discrimination through a single lens; instead, multiple identities can compound the effects of oppression. For Dalit women, their social positioning at the intersection of caste and gender leads to a compounded form of discrimination. The caste system, deeply entrenched in Indian society, demarcates individuals based on birth, with Dalits at the bottom of the hierarchy. At the same time, women in India face gender-based challenges irrespective of their caste. When these two forms of oppression intersect, Dalit women face unique challenges in accessing and thriving in higher education.

THE INTERSECTIONAL BARRIERS CONFRONTING DALIT WOMEN IN HIGHER EDUCATION

India's higher education system, long touted as a bastion of opportunity and social mobility, has in reality been plagued by deep-rooted inequities that systematically exclude and marginalize certain communities. Among the most vulnerable and disadvantaged in this context are Dalit women - those who bear the burden of both caste and gender-based oppression.

As members of the historically oppressed Dalit community and the female sex, Dalit women encounter a unique set of intersectional challenges that obstruct their access to and success in institutions of higher learning. These barriers, rooted in the interplay of casteism and patriarchy, manifest in multifaceted ways, erecting formidable obstacles to Dalit women's educational advancement and social mobility.

Legacies of Exclusion: Caste, Gender, and Educational Deprivation

The foundations of Dalit women's educational marginalization can be traced back to India's entrenched caste hierarchy and patriarchal social structures. Historically, the Dalit community, considered "untouchable," was denied access to formal schooling and knowledge systems - a means of maintaining the hegemony of the upper-caste elite. And within the Dalit community, women faced an additional layer of oppression, being relegated to the lowest rung of the social order (Rege, 1998).

This legacy of exclusion has persisted into the contemporary era, with Dalit women continuing to lag behind their upper-caste and male counterparts in educational attainment. National data reveals that while the overall female literacy rate in India stands at 65.5%, for Dalit women it plummets to a mere 54.6% (Government of India, 2011). Similarly, Dalit women's enrolment in higher education institutions remains abysmally low, with only 15.9% of Dalit women having access to college or university education compared to 29.4% of their male Dalit peers and 37.6% of upper-caste women (Ministry of Human Resource Development, 2018).

The reasons underlying these stark disparities are multifaceted and rooted in the intersections of caste and gender. Foremost among them is the economic deprivation that disproportionately afflicts Dalit households, forcing many Dalit girls to drop out of school and pursue income-generating work to support their families (Thapar-Björkert & Sanghera, 2016). Compounding this is the perpetuation of patriarchal norms that prioritize the education of sons over daughters, relegating Dalit women to the domestic sphere and denying them the same opportunities as their male counterparts.

Navigating Hostile Campus Climates

Even for the small proportion of Dalit women who do manage to access higher education, the journey is far from smooth. They often find themselves navigating hostile and unwelcoming campus environments dominated by privileged upper-caste students and faculty. Instances of overt caste-based discrimination, microaggressions, and social ostracization are rampant, creating a climate of alienation and exclusion for Dalit women (Rao, 2003).

These challenges are exacerbated by the lack of institutional support and representation within the higher education system. Many universities and colleges, rooted in Brahminical and patriarchal values, lack adequate representation of Dalit faculty and administrators. This not only deprives Dalit students of crucial mentors and role models but also perpetuates a curriculum and pedagogy that fails to acknowledge or address the realities of Dalit women's lived experiences (Guru, 1995).

Furthermore, the implementation of affirmative action policies and schemes intended to promote Dalit access to education has often been tokenistic and half-hearted, falling short of truly empowering this marginalized community. The deeply entrenched biases and resistance to change within the higher education establishment continue to undermine the efficacy of these measures, further

Intersectional Oppression of Dalit Women

Dalit women fall under this category; existing in the Indian subcontinent, they have unique lived experiences, as this faction is comprised of the intersectional oppressions of two groups both oppressed on account of their birth i. e., being Dalits and women. The doubly marginalized status of these women makes them a separate category whose experience of being Dalit women cannot be understood from the location of just being a Dalit or only a woman. It includes the interrelations and interactions of these two identities which reinforce each other. As a result, the awareness of Dalit women's issues has neither been addressed by mainstream feminism nor by the Dalit literary movement, which has been largely patriarchal. They remain in the category of "outsider within".

Women of the Dalit community endure the burden of multiple oppressions of caste, class, and gender. However, caste remains the main root of their sufferings. The caste system is an evil practice, and it is prohibited by the constitution of India yet persists in Indian society because it is so deeply ingrained in the minds of the people and thrives on social norms and ideologies. The Indian caste system is a social hierarchy, a closed society, in which the position and status of the individual in the society is decided by birth. The notion of 'purity and pollution' (unclean) and 'endogamy' (marriage within caste) are its characteristics. Caste has both religious and political derivation and demeanour. Socio-religious Hindu stratification of society gave rise to the Varna (order/colour/class) system. The Hindu social order, according to the holy texts, consists of a fourfold Varna-based society. The highest is that of the Brahmins (priests and teachers), below them the Kshatriyas (rulers and warriors), then the Vaishyas (traders and merchants), and finally the Shudras (servants), who did menial jobs for the other three Varnas. The Varna system was unique in its nexus of inherent caste and class structures. A person's occupation was inextricably linked with the caste identity. Foregrounding the class divisions embedded within the caste system, Marx and Engels (1845-46: 63) observed that the crude form of the division of labour found among the Indians called forth the caste system. They criticized the idealist belief that the caste system produced the crude form of division of labour. Thus, for Marx (1846: 158), the caste regime was also a particular division of labour (qt Bapuji 2009: 340-341). Louis Dumont states, "There is in actual fact a fifth category, the untouchables, who are left outside classification" (1999, 66-67). They are called "Varna's" or 'outcastes. ' They perform menial and impure work and hence are considered polluted and relegated to a peripheral existence in the casteist society. Historically they were referred to as 'Untouchables,' and called the 'Depressed classes,' 'Harijans,' and 'Dalit,' which is their cultural and political identity and also "a symbol of change and revolution" (Zelliot 1996: 268). In the 1930s, Ambedkar spearheaded a revolutionary movement that denounced the established norms and ideology of the caste Hindus. The movement interrogated the validity of the caste system based on which Hindus in India were socially stratified. Dalits articulated their dissent against the dominant ideology not only in social and political platforms but also through literary forms. Literature became an effective tool to express their protest and anguish against the domination of the Caste Hindus. As an arm of the Dalit liberation movement, Dalit literature not only reveals the angst of being a Dalit in a caste driven society, it also simultaneously registers a revolutionary discourse that challenges the hegemonic caste structures of the society (Geetha, 2011). Therefore, the Dalit literary movement is not purely a literary movement but also a "social movement for the liberation of Dalits and to bring about fundamental changes in the Indian social order" (Bhoite and Bhoite 1977: 74). The bourgeoning of Dalit literature began in the 1960s in Maharashtra, spread to other regions, and is now established as a pan Indian genre. While Dalit literature portrays the debased existence of Dalits, the representation foregrounds Dalit males as protagonists, the central figures of the suffering, subjugating women's miseries, struggles, endurance, and their roles in the community. Akin to a system of graded inequalities within the caste system, there are multiple "graded patriarchies" structured within the Hindu society (Chakravarti 2018: 79). While Brahminical patriarchy is at the top of this hierarchy, there are different forms of women's oppression, with specific gender and social norms functioning within each caste community. Hence, women's oppression is not unitary in Indian society, and women submit to the gender norms of their respective caste. As a result, the sufferings of the upper-caste women are different from those of the lower caste. The former generally suffer only gender-based oppression. They experience gender discrimination and domestic violence which may be related to gendered domestic labour, dowry, female infanticide, and "honour killing". On the contrary, the lower social, political, and economic status of Dalit women makes them undergo the rigidities of double patriarchal oppression. One is intrinsic patriarchy, which is the oppression of Dalit women by the men of their community. They are taxed, abused, and beaten by the men within the families. The second is the extrinsic patriarchy, which is the oppression and exploitation of Dalit women by the men of dominant castes. They experience economic and labour exploitation and also endure violence by men of the dominant castes. They suffer from constant threats of sexual molestation and rape. Uma Chakravarti proclaims, "Upper-caste men have had sexual access to lower caste women, an aspect of the material power they have over the lower castes" (2018: 81). They are thus victims of intersectional oppression of caste, class, and gender, which are interlocking in nature (Sharma and Kumar 2020). They are also the victims of religious practices such as Devadasis 7 and muralis8 /joginis9 (Geetha, 2021).

Therefore, it would be appropriate to say that issues of Dalit women are social rather than personal. Their problems remain unaddressed in the mainstream Indian feminist movement that was largely initiated by women from the dominant castes. Their resistance towards patriarchal structures was confined to their personal experiences of gender oppression. They failed to address the specific problems of women of the Dalit community related to caste discrimination, poverty, hunger, public violence, and sexual exploitation. The intersectional oppression, struggles, endurance, and contributions of Dalit women were also marginalized within the patriarchal Dalit political and literary movement, and thus they remain "outsiders within. " The masculinization of the Dalit movement and the Savaranisation of womanhood led to an exclusion of Dalit women from this movement and subjected them to interlocking oppressions of caste, class, and gender (Rege 2003: 91). The exclusion of Dalit women from both the mainstream feminist and Dalit movement led to the emergence of a Dalit feminist movement in the 1990s.

The "outsider within" status of Dalit women bestow them with a sort of double vision as living on the edge of society makes them conscious of patterns of social constructions that may not be comprehensible to sociological insiders: "I am speaking from a place in the margins where I am different, where I see things differently" (hooks 1990: 208). Similarly, the marginal location of Dalit women helps them to understand that advantaged groups use strategies and ideologies to restrict them to the periphery, thus limiting their access to societal resources and institutions that control, define, and relegate them. Therefore, they began voicing their collective issues both in writings as well as through Dalit Women Organizations and activism.

The experiences of Dalit women in higher education are a testament to their resilience and determination in the face of intersectional oppression. Despite the complex web of caste, gender, and class-based discrimination, Dalit women continue to navigate and challenge the systems of power that seek to marginalize them. Their stories of struggle and triumph serve as a powerful reminder of the need for inclusive and equitable education, one that values and centres the voices and perspectives of the most marginalized. As we move forward, it is essential that we prioritize the empowerment and liberation of Dalit women, recognizing their agency and autonomy as key drivers of social change. Only then can we hope to create a more just and equitable society, where Dalit women can thrive and reach their full potential."

CHAPTER 4

CONSTITUTIONAL SAFEGUARDS

CHAPTER 4

CONSTITUTIONAL SAFEGUARDS

Dalit Women in Higher Education: Empowerment through B.R. Ambedkar's Vision

Dalit women in India have long endured the dual burdens of caste and gender discrimination, which have obstructed their access to higher education and opportunities for advancement. However, the constitutional provisions and safeguards inspired by the visionary leader B.R. Ambedkar offer a path towards equality and justice, empowering Dalit women to pursue education as a means of liberation and social change.

Fundamental Rights and Equality

B.R. Ambedkar emphasized the foundational importance of equality in education for dismantling caste-based oppression. His vision, reflected in Article 15(1) of the Constitution, ensures that Dalit women are treated equally in educational institutions, regardless of their caste or gender.

Affirmative Action and Reservations

Ambedkar advocated for affirmative action as a necessary measure to uplift marginalize communities, including Dalit women. Article 15(4) of the Constitution reflects this vision by allowing for special provisions to advance the educational interests of Scheduled Castes, ensuring opportunities through reservations in educational institutions.

"I measure the progress of a community by the degree of progress which women have achieved." - B.R. Ambedkar

Directive Principles of State Policy

Article 46 embodies Ambedkar's commitment to addressing the educational and economic disparities faced by Dalit women. This directive principle mandates the state to promote their educational interests, acknowledging the transformative power of education in achieving social justice.

"Cultivation of mind should be the ultimate aim of human existence." - B.R. Ambedkar

Legal Safeguards and Protection

Ambedkar's advocacy for the rights and dignity of marginalized communities finds resonance in legislative protections such as the **Scheduled Castes and Scheduled Tribes (Prevention of Atrocities) Act, 1989**. This law safeguards Dalit women from discrimination and atrocities, ensuring a secure environment conducive to pursuing their educational aspirations.

"I measure the progress of a community by the degree of progress which women have achieved." - B.R. Ambedkar

Empowerment through Education

Education, according to Ambedkar is the cornerstone of empowerment and social transformation. By ensuring equitable access to higher education for Dalit women, constitutional safeguards inspired by Ambedkar pave the way for their socio-economic upliftment and active participation in nation-building efforts.

The constitutional safeguards rooted in B R Ambedkar's vision represent India's commitment to fostering equality, justice, and inclusivity for Dalit women in higher education. These provisions not only protect against discrimination but also promote affirmative action measures that are essential for expanding opportunities and representation in educational institutions. Through the transformative power of education, Dalit women can break barriers, challenge stereotypes, and contribute meaningfully to the progress of society.

As we continue to uphold Ambedkar's ideals and principles, India reaffirms its dedication to creating a more equitable and inclusive educational landscapes where every Dalit woman can thrive, succeed, and fulfil her potential. These constitutional safeguards serve as a testament to our collective pursuit of a society free from caste and gender-based discrimination, guided by the enduring legacy of B R Ambedkar.

The constitutional safeguards for Dalit women in higher education reflect India's commitment to promoting equality, justice, and inclusive development. These provisions not only protect against discrimination but also pave the way for affirmative action measures that are essential for expanding opportunities and representation in educational institutions.

CHAPTER 5

SIGINIFICANCE OF STUDY

CHAPTERE 5

SIGINIFICANCE OF STUDY

Need and Significance of Study

The present studies show how Dalit women are facing challenges to access higher education. Two major concerns were significantly highlighted concerning increased dropout rates among Dalit women in higher education. to know the social barriers faced by Dalit women and to identify issues and challenges faced by Dalit women in higher education. These were poverty and caste, and class barriers. Both these factors hurt the higher education of Dalit women. In addition to the obstacles that have been described above, it is difficult for Dalit women to get entrance to higher education. As Simon Chauchard (2014) pointed out in his discussion, Caste stigma also plays a vital role in the lack behind them. Dalit girls are forced to make sacrifices in their education at the request of their parents because they are reduced to a low social status as a result of a long-standing gender bias. This causes the girls to be condemned to a poor social status. Even the findings of older studies have been called into doubt. The results of the present study are supported by research, which also highlights the significance of the fact that the socialization process has a considerable impact on the education female's identity might be affected by parenting styles that are considered to be regressive.

Girls who do not get enough emotional care from their parents are more likely to experience mental stress and despair (Froerer, 2012, p. 347). The study highlights that most of the Dalit women do not have access to higher education. Either they are restricted or their socio-economic conditions make their existence difficult. Suffering from unemployment and liminal living standards force them to choose one year professional courses or other daily wage jobs in order to support their family financially. This study recounts the real life situations of Dalit women who are doubly marginalized and strives hard to find an identity and existence in the highly challenging world.

Significance of the study

To understand the complex experiences of Dalit women in higher education, who face multiple forms of oppression and marginalization. To highlight the intersectional nature of oppression, which is often overlooked in studies that focus on single aspects of identity. To provide a platform for Dalit women's voices and perspectives, which are often silenced or erased in dominant narratives. To inform inclusive and equitable policies and practices in higher education, addressing the specific needs and challenges of Dalit women. To contribute to the broader struggle for social justice and human rights, recognizing the interconnectedness of oppressions and the need for collective action.

Need of the study

There is a lack of research and data on the experiences of Dalit women in higher education, particularly in the context of intersectional oppression. Existing studies often focus on single aspects of identity, neglecting the complex intersections of caste, gender, class, and other factors. Dalit women's voices and perspectives are often absent from policy-making and decision-making processes in higher education. There is a need for inclusive and equitable policies and practices that address the specific needs and challenges of Dalit women in higher education. The study can help to inform and shape the broader discourse on social justice and human rights, highlighting the importance of intersectionality and collective action.

By studying the intersectional oppression of Dalit women in higher education, we can gain a deeper understanding of the complex challenges they face and work towards creating a more inclusive and equitable education system that values and empowers all individuals.

CHAPTER 6

METHODOLOGICAL FRAMEWORK OF RESEARCH

CHAPTER 6
METHODOLOGICAL FRAMEWORK OF RESEARCH

Exploring the Intersectional Lens of Dalit Women in Higher Education: Methodological Reflections and Findings from My Dissertation

Introduction

My dissertation conducted an in-depth analysis of the experiences of Dalit women in higher education through an intersectional lens. The term 'intersectionality,' first coined by Kimberlé Crenshaw, helped to frame the ways in which overlapping identities of caste, gender, class, and other social markers shape the unique challenges and experiences faced by Dalit women. This approach allowed me to examine the multifaceted barriers they encounter and offered insights into the resilience and agency they exhibit in navigating these adversities.

Research is a systematic attempt to obtain answer to meaningful question about phenomena or events through the application of scientific procedures. Research directed toward the solution of a problem. It may be understood as a science of studying how research is done scientifically. It is necessary for the research to know not only the research methods techniques but also the methodology (C R Kothari, 2007).

Statement of the Problem

Education is considered as an instrument of social change, individual mobility and social equality. It is a basic human right, embedded with a liberating potential and is chosen tool for contesting structures of inequality rooted in caste, class and gender. Indian society is characterized by division of caste, class, religion, region and gender while caste is a pervasive parameter and gives a hierarchical structure to the society. A section of the society continuously lacks opportunity to participate and benefit fully from society reflecting multiple overlapping natures of disadvantages experienced by certain groups, where social identity is the axis of exclusion (Kabeer, 2006)

Dalit's are the most deprived sections of Indian society and have been the victims of untouchability, segregation and denial of access to multiple resources. The constitutional provisions recognize the caste inequalities and provide ameliorative measures and opportunities towards inclusiveness. Education represents one way to break out of cycles of poverty and distress. Since independence, the statistics show a steady growth in the enrolment of Dalits at all levels of education but reveal unequal educational achievements. They also experience alienation, disempowerment, drop early, fail or leave with a lower degree qualification in the process of educational attainment. Hence not just enrolment but sustenance in the program and deriving meaningful benefits through education deserves to be the targeted goal.

Gender plays a crucial role in determining the chances of acquiring literacy and attaining higher educational qualification. Dalit women are the most marginalized among marginalized groups and face multiple forms of discrimination as members of impoverished class and as women. Their educational levels are considerably low in comparison to Dalits in general and non-Dalits in particular (Harinath, 2011) and especially in relation to higher education (Chanana, 2012). Dalit women face the triple jeopardy of oppression by caste, class and gender dominated by 'discrete' and 'overlapping' patriarchy. As a result of the systematic, entrenched and significant gender discrimination, Dalit women remain highly disadvantaged largely outside the reach of government policies. Hardly any research exists on SC women attaining higher education (Velaskar, 2010; Paik, 2014). To understand what operates in their access to higher education, reviews document individual histories, 'family habitus' (Coleman, 1990), access to 43 'cultural capital' (Bourdieu, 1977) and 'institutional habitus' (Reay et al., 2005) as important factors. Since such attempts are few in Indian context and in the academic field, the present study finds it as a necessary and researchable topic to be explored and explained.

In spite of state initiated programs, access to higher education remains a core issue for the Dalit community, especially girls. A range of socio-political, cultural, religious and economic factors are closely linked to low literacy levels and enrolment in higher education. A considerable progress is evident at all levels of education but the required momentum to gain from the affirmative action and prominent gender differences prompt to understand the complexities beneath. Several research studies exist on gender and education (Duraisamy, 2002 and Dutta, 2006) but fewer studies focus on issues related to access to higher education by caste and gender at a national level and at other cultural settings. An attempt is made in this study to trace the factors associated with access to higher education for Dalit women with focus on Parental Involvement, affordability, awareness of government schemes and support network.

DATA

30 Dalit women living in panchayath were taken as sample for study. Stratified random sampling method was used for data collection. The Dalit women belonged to 15-30 age group. I utilized stratified random sampling to select participants who identified as Dalit women and were currently enrolled in or had recently graduated from higher education institutions. This approach ensured that my sample was representative of the diversity within the Dalit community, considering factors such as geographical location, field of study, socioeconomic background, and educational attainment. I aimed to include voices from rural settings to provide a holistic view of their experiences. Based on the nature of the problem and objectives, the data was selected for the study. The data consist of 30 Dalit Women respondents from panchayath. Tool of Studies at

micro level can provide deeper insights for further research and address issues at a policy level. The study is descriptive in nature and qualitative approach.

In this chapter explains in detail the research problem, the tool used to collect data, techniques and method's used for the completion of this study. The researcher depended both on primary and secondary sources of data. The methodology is qualitative in nature. Semi Structured interview schedule was used to collect data from Dalit women. secondary sources of data were collected from written materials like books, journals articles and Gender Status Report of the particular panchayth. Although this work has extensively used semi structured interview schedule as the tool for collecting primary data and conduct interview with the Dalit women. In this interview schedule question belonging to problem faced by Dalit women, status of their education and to analyse about the intersectional oppression faced in higher education.

Data Collection Procedure

A panchayath was selected as the area of study. From this area 30 women were selected as sample. The interview was administrated in the concerned households. The investigator met the respondents at their residence to collect data and the interview was administrated to respondents personally.

Data Analysis

The collected data was analysed using qualitative method. The analysis helped the researcher to understand the perception of Dalit's women's higher Education status.

Conclusion

In this chapter include methodology related to research study. The chapter shows the sample, tool, data collection procedure, analysis etc.

CHAPTER 7
DATA-DRIVEN INSIGHTS

CHAPTER 7
DATA-DRIVEN INSIGHTS

Despite income improvements, persistent barriers such as caste-based discrimination, inadequate policy implementation, and systemic biases continue to impact Dalit women's access to education. The analysis highlights the need for targeted interventions to address financial barriers at each income level. These include increasing awareness and accessibility of scholarships, improving infrastructure, and implementing effective government policies. Establishing holistic support systems that address both financial and socio-cultural barriers can significantly improve educational outcomes for Dalit women.

The educational choices of Dalit women often reflect a pragmatic approach influenced by socio-economic factors and the pressing need for immediate employment opportunities. This discussion explores why Dalit women tend to prefer professional courses over higher education and the implications of this trend. This in-depth examination of our data provides a nuanced understanding of the intersectional barriers faced by Dalit women in higher education.

The following are the analysis realised a significant finding regarding the impact of intersectional oppression on Dalit women's academic outcomes. By analysing the data, the study demonstrated a clear correlation between experiences of marginalisation and reduced academic achievement.

The analysis realised a profound understanding of the intersectional obstacles faced by Dalit women in higher education.

Social and Cultural Factors

"The barriers that stand in the way of Dalit women's education are not just structural, but also social and cultural." - Ruth Manorama

There can be social pressure within Dalit communities to prioritize immediate financial contribution to the family over long-term educational goals. Professional courses meet this expectation by enabling quicker workforce entry (Shah, 2001). Traditional gender roles and responsibilities often pressure Dalit women to balance education with household duties. Professional courses, which require less time than higher education degrees, are more compatible with these roles (Paik, 2014).

Dalit women face discrimination and marginalization due to their low social status. They are often viewed as impure and untouchable, making it difficult for them to overcome the social stigma. This discrimination is perpetuated by societal norms and beliefs, making it essential to address these socio-cultural factors.

Addressing Socio-Cultural Factors

To address the socio-cultural factors that perpetuate discrimination and inequality, it is essential to create an inclusive and supportive environment. This requires policymakers and educators to work together to promote access to higher education for Dalit women.Policies and programs must prioritize access to higher education for Dalit women. This includes providing scholarships, mentorship programs, and counseling services to support their academic and personal growth.

Government and Institutional Support

While there are scholarships and financial aid programs available for higher education, awareness and accessibility issues persist. On the other hand, there is often more targeted support for vocational and professional training programs for marginalized communities (Jenkins, 2004). Policies aimed at promoting vocational training and professional education for Dalits are more robust and easier to access compared to those supporting higher education (Thorat & Newman, 2007).

Dalit women often face systemic discrimination in higher education institutions, including biases from faculty and peers. This hostile environment can deter them from pursuing higher education (Subramanian, 2015). Many higher education institutions lack the necessary infrastructure and support systems to accommodate the unique needs of Dalit women, such as mentorship programs and financial support (Deshpande, 2011). There is often a perception that higher education does not necessarily guarantee better job prospects, especially given the discrimination Dalit women might face in the professional world. Professional courses are seen as more directly linked to employment (Guru, 2009). There are more visible success stories of Dalit individuals who have taken professional courses and found stable employment, providing role models for young Dalit women to follow (Srinivas, 2002).

There needs to be a concerted effort to increase awareness about the availability of scholarships and financial aid for higher education among Dalit communities, Establishing mentorship programs that connect Dalit women with role models who have succeeded in higher education can provide encouragement and guidance. Policies aimed at supporting Dalit women's access to higher education need to be strengthened and effectively implemented. This includes financial aid, quotas, and anti-discrimination measures. Higher education institutions must undertake reforms to create a more inclusive and supportive environment for Dalit women, addressing both systemic discrimination and practical barriers. Developing educational programs that combine professional training with pathways to higher education can provide Dalit women with both immediate job skills and the opportunity for academic advancement. Offering flexible learning options such as part-time courses, online education, and vocational programs integrated with higher education can help Dalit women balance their educational aspirations with economic and social responsibilities

The preference for professional courses over higher education among Dalit women is a multifaceted issue driven by economic, social, and institutional factors. Addressing these challenges requires comprehensive strategies that enhance access to higher education, provide financial support, and create inclusive environments. By understanding and addressing the reasons behind this preference, policymakers and educators can better support the educational and professional aspirations of Dalit women.

The hidden hurdle: unfamiliarity with entrance examinations

The Common University Entrance Test (CUET) and the Central Universities Common Admission Test (CUCAT) are crucial examinations for gaining admission into undergraduate and postgraduate programs in central universities across India. However, there is a significant lack of awareness about these exams among Dalit women, which hampers their access to higher education. This discussion explores the reasons behind this lack of awareness, its implications, and possible solutions. socio-economic Barriers are Limited Access to Information.

Dalit women often reside in rural or economically disadvantaged areas with limited access to digital resources and the internet. This digital divide restricts their ability to obtain information about CUET and CUCAT exams (Desai & Kulkarni, 2008). Schools and colleges in areas with high Dalit populations often lack the infrastructure to provide adequate career counselling and information about higher education opportunities (Nambissan, 2009). Economic Constrains like costs associated with preparing for these exams, including coaching classes, study materials, and application fees, can be prohibitive for many Dalit families. This financial barrier contributes to a lack of awareness and participation (Thorat & Newman, 2007).

Gender and caste Discrimination is a prevailing social attitude, and caste-based discrimination often discourages Dalit women from pursuing higher education. Families may prioritise immediate income generation over education for their daughters (Paik, 2014). Traditional gender roles often place domestic responsibilities on Dalit women, limiting their time and focus on educational pursuits (Rege, 2006). There is a scarcity of Dalit women in higher education and professional fields, resulting in a lack of role models who can inspire and guide younger generations (Shah, 2001). The absence of mentorship programmes within Dalit communities means that many young women do not receive the guidance needed to navigate the complexities of higher education entrance exams (Jodhka & Newman, 2010).

Government and educational institutions often fail to effectively reach out to marginalised communities to provide information about CUET and CUCAT. This lack of targeted outreach results in Dalit women remaining uninformed about these opportunities (Jenkins, 2004). Existing awareness programmes are often not tailored to address the specific needs and circumstances of Dalit women, leading to inadequate dissemination of information (Subramanian, 2015). Language barriers are the main issue faced by them. Information about CUET and CUCAT is frequently disseminated in English or Hindi, which may not be the primary languages for many Dalit women, especially in rural areas (Deshpande, 2011). Educational campaigns often fail to engage with community leaders and grassroots organisations that could effectively spread awareness within Dalit communities (Guru, 2009).

The lack of awareness about CUET and CUCAT examinations perpetuates educational inequality, as Dalit women miss out on opportunities to enter central universities, which offer better resources and academic environments (Nambissan, 2009). the employment opportunities Limited access to higher education restricts Dalit women's career prospects and economic mobility, reinforcing cycles of poverty and social exclusion (Desai & Kulkarni, 2008).

Higher education is a critical pathway to social and economic empowerment. The lack of awareness about entrance exams like CUET and CUCAT undermines efforts to uplift Dalit women and integrate them into mainstream society (Paik, 2014). The barriers faced by Dalit women in accessing higher education are multifaceted and deeply rooted in systemic inequalities. Discrimination based on caste, gender, and socio-economic status often intersects to create significant hurdles for Dalit women seeking higher education opportunities. One major barrier is the lack of access to quality primary and secondary education due to socio-economic disadvantages and discrimination within the education system This sets the foundation for the educational inequality that persists in higher education. Research by Thorat and Attewell

(2007) found that Dalit women are disproportionately represented among dropouts at various levels of education, highlighting the challenges they face in completing their education. Additionally, they often lack the financial resources and family support necessary to pursue higher education.

Further compounding these challenges are social stigmas and stereotypes that perpetuate low expectations for Dalit women's educational attainment. Discrimination and harassment within academic institutions also create hostile environments that deter Dalit women from pursuing higher education or completing their studies. Efforts to address these barriers must include targeted policies and interventions aimed at addressing the intersecting forms of discrimination faced by Dalit women. This could involve providing scholarships, mentorship programmes, and support services tailored to their needs, as well as implementing anti-discrimination measures within educational institutions.

Overall, addressing the barriers faced by Dalit women in accessing higher education requires a comprehensive approach that addresses both systemic inequalities and the specific challenges they face within the education system.

Socio-Economic Factors faced by Dalit women

Dalit women in India face a multitude of socioeconomic barriers that hinder their ability to access and succeed in higher education. Despite efforts to promote inclusivity and equality, these women continue to confront entrenched obstacles that perpetuate their marginalization and exclusion.One of the primary barriers is caste-based discrimination, which manifests in various forms, including bias, prejudice, and stereotypes. Dalit women are often subjected to a hostile learning environment, where they are made to feel inferior and unwelcome. This can lead to a sense of isolation and exclusion, making it difficult for them to succeed academically.

Financial constraints are another significant obstacle that Dalit women face. Limited access to financial resources and scholarships means that many are unable to afford the costs associated with higher education. This forces them to rely on family support or take on part-time jobs, which can compromise their academic performance. Social exclusion is another significant barrier that Dalit women face. They are often excluded from social and academic networks, which limits their access to opportunities and resources. This can make it difficult for them to find mentors, internships, and job opportunities, further marginalizing them.

"THE AFFORDABLITY GAP: WHEN FAMILY RESOURCES FALL SHORT"

Research shows that family affordability plays a crucial role in enabling Dalit women to pursue higher education. According to a study conducted by Khalid and Desai (2016), financial constraints are one of the primary barriers preventing Dalit women from accessing higher education opportunities. The study highlights how poverty and economic marginalisation within Dalit communities often limit families' ability to support their daughters' educational aspirations. According to research conducted in particular panchayth many Dalit families struggle to afford basic necessities, let alone the high costs associated with higher education, such as tuition fees, textbooks, and living expenses. Furthermore, Dalit women are more likely to come from families with lower levels of educational attainment and income, exacerbating the financial barriers they face in accessing higher education. To address these challenges, targeted interventions are needed to alleviate the financial burden on Dalit families and support Dalit women in pursuing higher education. This could involve providing scholarships, grants, or financial assistance specifically tailored to the needs of Dalit women. This discussion explores the broader implications, contextualises the findings with existing literature, and suggests actionable steps.

"THE ROLE MODEL VACCUM: A BARRIER TO SUCCESS"

The lack of role models and mentors is another significant obstacle. The scarcity of Dalit women in academia means that there are limited role models and mentors to inspire and guide them. This can make it difficult for them to navigate the academic system and access resources and opportunities.

Family and societal expectations also play a significant role in limiting Dalit women's access to higher education. They are often expected to prioritize family obligations over education, perpetuating gender and caste stereotypes.

This can lead to a sense of guilt and responsibility, making it difficult for them to pursue their academic goals.

Limited access to resources

Limited access to resources is another significant barrier. Schools and colleges in marginalized areas often lack adequate infrastructure, libraries, and technology, making it difficult for Dalit women to access quality education.

Limited access to healthcare

Health and well-being are also significant concerns for Dalit women. Limited access to healthcare, sanitation, and nutrition means that they are more likely to experience poor health and well-being, which can compromise their academic performance.

Intersectional identity is another critical factor that Dalit women face. They experience multiple forms of discrimination based on their caste, gender, class, and other identities, which can further marginalize them.

Finally, limited representation is a significant obstacle that Dalit women face. They are underrepresented in higher education and academia, which perpetuates their invisibility and silences their voices.

Despite these obstacles, Dalit women in higher education demonstrate remarkable resilience and resistance. They challenge the status quo and pave the way for future generations. However, it is essential to address and overcome these barriers to promote inclusivity and empowerment.

Dalit women in higher education face a multitude of socioeconomic barriers that hinder their ability to access and succeed in higher education. Addressing these barriers is essential to promote inclusivity and empowerment. This requires policies and initiatives that address caste-based discrimination, financial constraints, social exclusion, lack of role models and mentors, family and societal expectations, limited access to resources, health and well-being, intersectional identity, and limited representation. By promoting inclusivity and empowerment, we can create a more equitable and just society where Dalit women can succeed and thrive.

"FROM BOOKS TO BREADWINNING: IMMEDIATE FINANCIAL RETURN"

Many Dalit families face significant financial hardships, necessitating quick entry into the job market. Professional courses, often shorter in duration compared to higher education degrees, offer a quicker pathway to employment and income generation (Nambissan, 2009)Financial Constraints also another reason. The high cost of higher education, including tuition fees, books, and living expenses, can be prohibitive. Professional courses, on the other hand, tend to be more affordable and provide a faster return on investment (Desai & Kulkarni, 2008).

JOB MARKET REALITIES: NAVIGATING THE CHALLENGES

Professional courses are often aligned with specific industries and job roles, making graduates more immediately employable. This is particularly important for Dalit women, who may face discrimination in the job market and need clear, direct pathways to employment (Jodhka & Newman, 2010). Many professional courses focus on practical skills and vocational training, which are highly valued in certain job sectors. This practical focus can make Dalit women more competitive candidates in the job market (Rege, 2006).

"BENEATH THE SURFACE": THE HIDDEN STRUGGLE OF EXTREME POVERTY

The research highlights a crucial finding of Extreme Poverty Income (Below 5,000) This sets the foundation for the educational inequality that persists in higher education. Research by Thorat and Attewell (2007) found that Dalit women are disproportionately represented among dropouts at various levels of education, highlighting the challenges they face in completing their education. Additionally, they often lack the financial resources and family support necessary to pursue higher education.

Further compounding these challenges are social stigmas and stereotypes that perpetuate low expectations for Dalit women's educational attainment. Discrimination and harassment within academic institutions also create hostile environments that deter Dalit women from pursuing higher education or completing their studies. Efforts to address these barriers must include targeted policies and interventions aimed at addressing the intersecting forms of discrimination faced by Dalit women. This could involve providing scholarships, mentorship programmes, and support services tailored to their needs, as well as implementing anti-discrimination measures within educational institutions.

Overall, addressing the barriers faced by Dalit women in accessing higher education requires a comprehensive approach that addresses both systemic inequalities and the specific challenges they face within the education system.

Research shows that family affordability plays a crucial role in enabling Dalit women to pursue higher education. According to a study conducted by Khalid and Desai (2016), financial constraints are one of the primary barriers preventing Dalit women from accessing higher education opportunities. The study highlights how poverty and economic marginalisation within Dalit communities often limit families' ability to support their daughters' educational aspirations. Many Dalit families struggle to afford basic necessities, let alone the high costs associated with higher education, such as tuition fees, textbooks, and living expenses. Furthermore, Dalit women are more likely to come from families with lower levels of educational attainment and income, exacerbating the financial barriers they face in accessing higher education. To address these challenges, targeted interventions are needed to alleviate the financial burden on Dalit families and support Dalit women in pursuing higher education. This could involve providing scholarships, grants, or financial assistance specifically tailored to the needs of Dalit women. This discussion explores the broader implications, contextualises the findings with existing literature, and suggests actionable steps.

Extreme Poverty Families in this income bracket face severe financial constraints, significantly limiting their ability to afford educational expenses such as tuition, books, and uniforms. This economic hardship results in high dropout rates among Dalit girls. Research by Thorat and Newman (2010) highlights that extreme poverty among Dalit households leads to compromised educational opportunities due to prioritising basic survival needs over schooling. Additionally, dependence on child labour further restricts educational pursuits, as young girls are often required to contribute to the family income.

The analysis brings to a hidden pattern of financial Strain Families with slightly higher incomes still experience substantial financial strain, balancing educational costs with other household expenses. This often results in students needing to take up part-time work, which negatively impacts their academic performance. According to Desai and Dubey (2012), financial instability in this income bracket often forces Dalit students to prioritise work over education, leading to inconsistent school attendance and higher dropout rates. High transportation costs to reach distant schools further exacerbate these challenges, making regular attendance difficult.

The analyses demonstrate moderate Financial Constraints Families While access to basic educational resources improves for families in this income range, significant financial pressures remain. The ability to invest in additional educational resources, such as tutoring, is limited. A study by Kumar (2016) indicates that even moderate financial stability does not eliminate the barriers to quality education for Dalit women, as systemic issues and social discrimination persist. Potential access to government educational support schemes exists, but bureaucratic hurdles often impede their effective utilization. Moreover, empowering Dalit women economically through skill development programmes, entrepreneurship initiatives, and job opportunities can help improve family affordability and create a conducive environment for higher education. Families in this income bracket face severe financial constraints, significantly limiting their ability to afford educational expenses such as tuition, books, and uniforms. This economic hardship results in high dropout rates among Dalit girls. Research by Thorat and Newman (2010) highlights that extreme poverty among Dalit households leads to compromised educational opportunities due to prioritising basic survival needs over schooling. Additionally, dependence on child labour further restricts educational pursuits, as young girls are often required to contribute to the family income.

This often results in students needing to take up part-time work, which negatively impacts their academic performance. According to Desai and Dubey

(2012), financial instability in this income bracket often forces Dalit students to prioritise work over education, leading to inconsistent school attendance and higher dropout rates. High transportation costs to reach distant schools further exacerbate these challenges, making regular attendance difficult.

CHAPTER 8

FINDINGS AND SUGGESTIONS

CHAPTER 8

FINDINGS AND SUGGESTIONS

In this chapter, the findings and suggestions investigates the intersectional oppression faced by Dalit women in higher education, exploring how the interplay of caste and gender exacerbates their marginalization. Through a qualitative approach, including interviews and surveys, the research identifies systemic discrimination, social barriers, and limited access to resources as critical factors hindering their educational experiences. The analysis reveals that the compounded effects of caste and gender significantly impede Dalit women's academic success and overall well-being. This study highlights the urgent need for policies and interventions that address these multifaceted challenges to ensure equitable access and opportunities for Dalit women in higher education. The findings contribute to the broader discourse on intersectionality and emphasize the importance of nuanced approaches in tackling educational inequities.

Objective Present Study was the Following

1. To know the social cultural barriers faced by Dalit women.
2. To identify issues and challenges faced by Dalit women in higher education.

Sample

The sample consist of 30 women in panchayath in were taken as sample for the study. Semi structured interview schedule was used for Data collection. The Dalit women belonged to 15-30 age group.

Tool for Data collection

The data was collected with the help of a semi structured interview schedule. for the purpose of the study, the interview schedule was developed with open ended question which were compiled in Malayalam. The information was collected from the question belonging to problem faced by Dalit women, to identify their issues and challenges and to identify social and economic barriers faced by Dalit women in higher education.

Data Collection Procedure

A panchayath was selected for the area of the study. From this area 30 women were selected as the sample. The interview was scheduled in concerned households. The investigator met the respondents at their residence to collect data and interview was administrated to the respondents personally. **Data analysis** In this study collected data was analyses qualitatively

Major Findings

This study revealed that the lower academic performance and limited access to higher education among Dalit women hinder their career prospects and economic development.

Due to financial constraints, Dalit girls in the panchayath invariably refrained from selecting hostel accommodations during their academic pursuits. They did not have an awareness program regarding the availability of scholarships and financial aid for higher education among Dalit women. Larger part did not participate in mentorship programs. Creating mentorship programs that link Dalit women with role models who have succeeded in higher education can offer encouragement and guidance. The majority of Dalit women lack awareness about the CUET and CUCAT examinations and limited family affordability. Greatest number of Dalit women have chosen their course of study based on their parents' and friends' preferences and lacked support from home.

Prevailing lacked educational resources, such as adequate study materials, internet access, and access to scholarships. Among the respondents, none completed education beyond graduation. A minority completed undergraduate studies, while the majority finished their plus-two education and opted for one-year professional courses like modest salary occupation. No Dalit women have taken any kind of loan from the government for their education. Most of Dalit women believe that education is very important for women. The majority encounter language barriers, with limited English proficiency posing the greatest challenge to their academic progress. There is a dearth of coaching institutes and inadequate study materials for central university examinations. Poverty is a major impediment, rendering higher education unaffordable. Financial aid, scholarships, and grants available to Dalit women are woefully insufficient. Educational infrastructure is substandard, with poor-quality schooling in Dalit-dominated areas undermining their readiness for higher education. Higher education institutions are sparsely available in panchayath, where many Dalit women reside. Institutions accessible to Dalit women are plagued by inadequate infrastructure, including deficient libraries, laboratories, and other essential resources. There is a notable lack of awareness among Dalit women regarding existing policies, scholarships, and affirmative action measures. The majority of Dalit women have not participated in any career guidance and counseling classes. A significant number of Dalit women actively engage in a variety of social, political, and cultural activities.

Language barriers have been a significant obstacle for Dalit women in Panchayat, hindering their access to education, employment, healthcare, and social services. Despite the country's linguistic diversity, the dominant languages of power and privilege have historically been Sanskrit, Hindi, and English, marginalizing the languages and dialects spoken by Dalit communities.

Dalit women's language and culture have been subjected to erasure and stigma, perpetuating their oppression. Their native languages, such as Bhojpuri, Maithili, and Telugu, are often considered "backward" or "unrefined," reinforcing the notion that Dalit languages and cultures are inferior. This linguistic marginalization has far-reaching consequences, including limited access to education, employment, and healthcare.

In education, Dalit women face language barriers that hinder their academic progress. The dominant language of instruction is often Hindi or English, which may not be their native language. This leads to a higher dropout rate among Dalit girls, perpetuating the cycle of poverty and illiteracy. Moreover, the curriculum rarely includes Dalit languages, literature, or history, erasing their cultural heritage and identity.

In the workplace, Dalit women encounter language barriers that limit their job opportunities and career advancement. Many industries prioritize proficiency in dominant languages, excluding Dalit women from employment opportunities. Furthermore, language barriers prevent Dalit women from accessing healthcare services, leading to poor health outcomes and reduced life expectancy.

Language barriers also perpetuate social exclusion and stigma. Dalit women's language and culture are often stigmatized, leading to a loss of cultural identity and heritage. The dominant languages and cultures are privileged, while

Dalit languages and cultures are marginalized, perpetuating the caste system's hierarchies.

To address these language barriers, initiatives such as language education programs, cultural revitalization efforts, and inclusive policymaking are essential. By promoting linguistic diversity and celebrating Dalit languages and cultures, we can work towards a more inclusive society where Dalit women's voices are valued and empowered.

Suggestions for Improving the Present Condition

1) To organise awareness programmes towards the importance of higher education.

2) Panchayath obliged coaching centres for central universities examinations.

3) Develop appropriate schemes and planning for social, economic development of Dalit women in panchayth.

4) Government agencies and NGO'S should be make awareness programmes about the right of women.

5) Organise awareness programmes about the proper use of stipends and scholarships of Dalit women student for their studies.

6) Enhanced outreach programs should implemented by Government to Inform Dalit communities about CUET and CUCAT exams, also utilizing common language and networks.

8) Universities and Colleges should partner with NGOs and community organizations to conduct awareness campaigns and workshop in panchayth.

9) Providing scholarships and financial subsidies for Dalit women to cover application fees and coaching expense can reduce economic barriers.

10) Providing information about CUET and CUCAT examinations in multilingual resources can ensure broader accessibility. utilizing community radio, local newspapers, and social media platforms to disseminate information about these exams can enhance awareness.

11) Establishing holistic support systems that address financial, social and emotional barriers can significantly improve educational outcomes. This includes improving school infrastructure, increasing awareness of available resources, and fostering an inclusive educational environment.

12) Expanding scholarships and financial aid programs specifically targeted at Dalit women is essential. These programs should be well-publicized within Dalit communities to ensure maximum awareness and uptake. Financial aid packages should cover not only tuition fees but also ancillary costs such as textbooks, accommodation, and transportation. Collaboration with non-profit organizations and private sectors to create scholarship funds can also amplify the resources available.

13) Government and private institutions should consider offering subsidized education for Dalit women. This can include reduced tuition fees, free hostel facilities, and provision of essential learning materials. Such subsidies can significantly alleviate the financial burden on Dalit families, making higher education more accessible.

14) Flexible employment opportunities within educational institutions can help Dalit women support their studies financially. Work-study programs, internships, and part-time jobs should be made available and promoted. These opportunities not only provide financial support but also offer valuable work experience that enhances employability post-graduation.

15) Effective community outreach programs are critical. Educational seminars and workshops should be conducted in Dalit communities to inform families about the benefits of higher education and available resources. Outreach efforts should involve local leaders and respected community members to build trust and credibility.

16) Providing career counseling and guidance services at the school level can help Dalit girls and their families understand the importance of higher education. These services should include information about various career options, the long-term benefits of higher education, and how to navigate the application and financial aid processes.

17) Strengthening the implementation and monitoring of affirmative action policies is crucial. Policies must be transparent, and their implementation should be regularly reviewed to ensure that they are genuinely benefiting Dalit women. Additionally, outreach programs should educate Dalit communities about these policies and how to avail themselves of them.

18) Educational institutions must foster an inclusive environment. Diversity training for faculty and students can help reduce bias and discrimination. Institutions should adopt strict anti-discrimination policies and create mechanisms for reporting and addressing grievances effectively.

19) Comprehensive are essential for Dalit women in higher education. This includes academic mentorship programs, mental health counselling, and peer support networks. Institutions should also provide tailored support for first-generation college students, helping them navigate the academic and social aspects of college life.

20) Creating safe spaces on campus where Dalit women can discuss their experiences, seek support, and build a community is important. These spaces should be free from discrimination and stigma, providing a sanctuary for marginalized students.

21) Engaging families and communities in discussions about the importance of educating women is crucial. Programs that highlight the successes of educated

Dalit women can shift perceptions and encourage more families to prioritize education for their daughters.

22) Highlighting successful Dalit women as role models can inspire and motivate young women. Mentorship programs connecting students with these role models can provide guidance, support, and a network of professional contacts.

23) Conducting regular research and collecting data on the educational experiences and outcomes of Dalit women is essential for informed policy-making. This data can help identify gaps, track progress, and refine programs to better meet the needs of Dalit women.

24) Monitoring and evaluating the impact of existing programs and policies is necessary to ensure they are effective. Regular assessments can help identify what works and what doesn't, allowing for continuous improvement.

25) Expanding access to online education and digital resources can provide flexible learning opportunities for Dalit women, especially those in remote or underserved areas. Online courses, virtual classrooms, and digital libraries can make higher education more accessible.

26) Developing and promoting e-learning platforms that offer courses, skill development programs, and certification can help Dalit women enhance their qualifications and employability without the constraints of traditional classroom settings.

27) Supporting and scaling up successful community-based initiatives that provide educational support and advocacy for Dalit women can have a significant impact. These programs often have a deep understanding of local needs and can provide tailored support.

28) Fostering partnerships with local NGOs, community organizations, and educational institutions can create a supportive network for Dalit women. These partnerships can provide resources, mentorship, and advocacy, helping to bridge the gap between policy and practice.

29) Implementing these suggestions requires a concerted effort from government bodies, educational institutions, non-profit organizations, and the communities themselves. A sustained commitment to equity and inclusion will be essential to bring about meaningful change in the higher education landscape for Dalit women.

30) The Common University Entrance Test (CUET) and the Central Universities Common Admission Test (CUCAT) are crucial examinations for gaining admission into undergraduate and postgraduate programs in central universities across India. However, there is a significant lack of awareness about these exams among Dalit women, which hampers their access to higher education. This discussion explores the reasons behind this lack of awareness, its implications, and possible solutions.

During the last sixty years the governments have been striving hard to redress the special grievances of Dalit women. However there is an urgent need to augment the process. Academicians, administrators, nongovernmental agencies and social reformers have suggested various approaches such as; development, enablement, empowerment and human rights approach and some of these have been experimented by the government without much success. However the situation is not beyond redemption. This modest study does not have any pretentions hazard remedial measures. However, the following suggestions to retrieve the situation would help administrators and policy makers.

Government should first evolve a clear vision about empowerment of Dalit women and set up a firm mission to deliver the goal. During the last sixty years it has been experimenting on models such as development, progress, growth, and enablement and at last empowerment. Frequent shifts in paradigms confuse the administrators and will scuttle the process. Hence, it is necessary to have clarity of the concept of empowerment. Equal access to education for Dalit women and girls must be ensured. Special measures should be taken to eliminate discrimination, universalize education, eradicate illiteracy, create a gender-sensitive educational system, increase enrolment and retention rates of girls and improve the quality of education to facilitate lifelong learning. Priority should be accorded to the development of occupation/vocation/technical skills by Dalit women. Reducing the gender gap in secondary and higher education could be a focus area. Sectoral time targets in existing policies must be achieved, with a special focus on women belonging to Scheduled Castes/Scheduled Tribes/Other Backward Classes/ Minorities. Gender sensitive curricula should be developed at all levels of educational system in order to address sex stereotyping as one of the causes of gender discrimination. Since Dalit women comprise the majority of the population below the poverty line and are very often in situations of extreme poverty, given the harsh realities of intra-household and social discrimination, macroeconomic policies and poverty eradication programmes should specifically address the needs and problems of such women. Dalit –women- oriented programmes should be designed with special targets. Steps should be taken for mobilization of poor women and convergence of services, by offering them a range of economic and social options, along with necessary support measures to enhance their capabilities. In view of the agriculture and allied sectors being their mainstay, concentrated efforts should be made to ensure that benefits of training, extension and various programmes will reach them in proportion to their numbers. The programmes for training women in soil conservation, social forestry, dairy development and other occupations allied to agriculture like horticulture, livestock including small animal husbandry, poultry, fisheries etc. should be expanded to benefit women workers in the agriculture sector. Progress has to be achieved in increasing recognition of the gender dimensions of poverty, and efforts should be made to mainstream a gender perspective into poverty eradication and programmes. Progress should be made by pursing a two-pronged approach of promoting employment and income income-generating activities for women In order to enhance women's access to credit for consumption and production and self employment, the establishment of new and strengthening of existing micro-credit mechanisms and micro-finance institution should be undertaken so that the outreach of credit should be enhanced. Other supportive measures would be taken to ensure adequate flow of credit through extant financial institutions and banks, so that Dalit women below poverty line have easy access to credit. Strengthening self-help groups.

Traditionally assigned gender roles have circumscribed Dalit women' Voices in education and careers and compel women to assume the burden for household responsibilities. All hindrances to economic and political career of Dalit women should be remained. National machineries must be instituted and recognized as the institutional base and catalysts for promoting gender equality, gender mainstreaming and monitoring of the implementation of the action plans. Legal reforms must immediately be undertaken and discriminatory provisions be eliminated in civil, penal and person status law governing marriage and family relations, women's property and ownership rights, and women's political work and employment rights. Steps should be taken to realize women's de facto enjoyment of their human rights through the creation of an enabling environment, including the adoption of policy measures, the improvement of enforcement and monitoring mechanisms and the implementation of legal literacy and awareness campaigns. A holistic approach to women's health which includes both nutrition and health services should be adopted and special attention be given to the needs of women and the girl at all stages of the life cycle.

An integrated approach was to be used for achieving women empowerment. This implied that the efforts made on various fronts like social, economic, legal and political would be harmonized. Further a strategy to earmark funds as "women's component" was to be adopted to ensure that the flow of resources was adequate. In this direction, the Tenth Plan has called for the expeditious adoption of the 'National Policy for Empowering Women' along with a well defined 'Gender Development Index' to monitor progress made towards improving women's status in the society.

Government should take the challenge of empowerment of Dalit women a as culmination point for the process of their empowerment. This process will help in identifying the areas to be targeted, planning the strategies for action and in the education evaluation of the outcomes. Empowerment cannot be a process either horizontal or vertical but could be a process which will go round in a circle. The beginning certainly ends in a change and sure for the better.

CONCLUSION

CONCLUSION

The journey of Dalit women in higher education is a testament to their resilience and determination. Despite the formidable barriers that stand in their way, they continue to strive for knowledge, equality, and empowerment. It is our collective responsibility to create a more inclusive and equitable society where Dalit women can access quality education, shatter the glass ceiling, and reach their full potential. By dismantling the socioeconomic barriers that have held them back for far too long, we can unlock their talents, unleash their creativity, and empower them to become agents of change. Together, let us build a brighter future where Dalit women can shine, succeed, and inspire future generations."

This research has revealed that a significant intersectional barrier faced by Dalit women in higher education is the lack of language proficiency, specifically in English, which is the dominant language of instruction in higher education. This language barrier prevents them from fully participating in career counselling classes, accessing resources, and receiving guidance that is essential for their academic and professional success. The lack of language proficiency is a result of the historical and systemic denial of access to quality education, particularly English language instruction, to marginalized communities like Dalit women. This perpetuates their marginalization and exclusion from opportunities and resources. To address this inequality, it is essential to provide language support services and career counseling programs that are optimized to the needs of Dalit women and other marginalized communities. This requires a commitment to creating inclusive and equitable higher education system, where language proficiency is not a barrier to success.

In conclusion, our exploration of education highlights the importance of recognizing and addressing the intersecting forms of oppression that marginalized students face. we can work towards creating a more inclusive and equitable education system that values and empowers all students. Let us strive to build a future where every student can thrive, regardless of their race, gender, sexual orientation, ability, or background. Together, we can create a world that is just, equitable, and intersectional in its approach to education and beyond. also emphasizes the importance of considering intersectionality in addressing the challenges faced by marginalized students in education. By recognizing the interconnected nature of different forms of oppression, we can work towards creating a more inclusive and equitable education system that values and empowers all students.

Savitribai Phule, a pioneering Indian educator and social reformer: 'Education is the right of every human being, and it is our collective responsibility to ensure that no one is denied this fundamental right.' May her words inspire us to action, as we strive to create a world where education is a powerful tool for empowerment, not a privilege reserved for the few. By empowering Dalit women through education, we can build a brighter future, where every individual can shine, succeed, and reach their full potential.

BIBLIOGRAPHY

BIBLIOGRAPHY

Abdul Salim, A., & Gopinathan Nair, P. R. (2002). *Educational development in India*: The Kerala experience since 1800. New Delhi: Anmol.

Alkire, Sabina (2007). Measuring Agency: Issues and Possibilities. *Indian Jour nal of Human Development*. Vol. 1(1).

Anand Jaya S. (2002). Self-Help Groups in Empowering Women: Case study of selected SHGs and NHGs, Discussion Paper No. 38. Kerala Research Programme on Local Level Development.

Arya, S., & Rathore, A. S. (Eds.). (2019). Dalit feminist theory: A reader. Taylor & Francis.

Asrani, S., & Kaushik, S. (2011). *Problems perceived by scheduled caste women in Haryana.* Studies of Tribes and Tribals, 9(1), 29-36.

Basu, Ramit (2010). The Role of the Gram Sabha in the process of planning - An analytical approach, Proceedings of the National Seminar on Grama sabha edited by S. A. Ashraful Hasan and G. S. Ganesh Prasad, Abdul Nazir Sab State Institute of Rural Development, Mysore Government of Karnataka

Bates Lisa M., Schuler Sidney Ruth & Islam Farzana. (2004). Socioeconomic factors and processes associated with domestic violence in rural Bangladesh. International Family Planning Perspectives. 30: 190-199.

Beecher, Catharine Esther & Beecher Stove Harriet (1869). *The American Women's Home*. NewYork, J. B. Ford Company.

Beteta Cueva, Hanny (2006). What is missing in measures of women's empowerment? *Journal of Human Development*. 7(2): 22141.

Bhagavatheeswaran, L., Nair, S., Stone, H., Isac, S., Hiremath, T., Raghavendra, T., ... & Beattie, T. S. (2016). The barriers and enablers to education among scheduled caste and scheduled tribe adolescent girls in northern Karnataka, South India: A qualitative study. *International journal of educational development,* 49, 262-270.

Biswas (1999). Measuring Women's empowerment some methodological issues. *Asia-Pacific Journal of Rural Development* Vol. 9, No. 2, P. 63-71.

Borah, Ajit (2014). Women empowerment through Self Help Groups-A case study of Barhampur Development Block in Nagaon District of Assam. *IOSR Journal of Economics and Finance* (IOSR-JEF) e-ISSN: 2321- 5933, p-ISSN: 2321-5925. 4 (3) 56-62.

Bui Chung, Daisy Kulvatee Kantachote, Asmah Mallick, Rachel Polster, Kelsey Roets (2013). Indicators of Women's Empowerment in Developing Nations, Paper presented in the Workshop in International Public Affairs, Robert M. La Follette School of Public Affairs.

Census 2011. Ministry of Statistics, Government of India.

Chanana, K. (1993). Accessing higher education: the dilemma of schooling women, minorities, Scheduled Castes and Scheduled Tribes in contemporary India. Higher Education, 26(1), 69-92.

Charmes J & Wieringa S. (2003). Measuring Women's Empowerment: An Assessment of the GenderRelated Development Index and the Gender Empowerment Measure. *Journal of Human Development* [serial online, 4(3): 419-435.

Chetia, Madhurya & Devajyoti Gogoi (2013), Empowerment of women through panchayathi raj system, *International Journal of Humanities and Social Science Invention* ISSN, 2(6), 05-09.

Das, Suchitra (2014). Women Participation in panchayathi Raj: A Case Study of Karimganj District of Assam, *International Journal of Humanities & Social Science Studies* (IJHSSS), Volume-I, Issue-I, pp 52- 58.

Deshpande, A., & Newman, K. (2007). Where the path leads: The role of caste in post-university employment expectations. *Economic and Political Weekly*, 42(41), 4133–4140.

Deshpande, S. (2006). Exclusive inequalities: Merit, caste and discrimination in Indian higher education today. *Economic and Political Weekly*, 41(24), 2438–2444.

Devaki, Jane (1990). Development, Theory and Practice, Insights Emer ging fr om Women's Experience. *Economic and Political Weekly*, 22(27), 1454-55.

Devi Lakshmy, K. R. (1996). Determinants of Labour Force Participation among Women in Kerala- Some Evidence from a Micro Level Study. *The Asian Economic Review*, 38(4).

Devi, Lakshmy, K. R. (2002). Education, Employment and Job preference of woman in Kerala: A micro level case study. Discussion paper No: 42, *Kerala Research Programme on Local level Development*, CDS, Trivandrum.

Dunn, D. (1993). Gender inequality in education and employment in the scheduled castes and tribes of India. *Population Research and Policy Review*, 12(1), 53-70.

Eapen, Mridual & Thomas, Soya (2005). Gender analysis of select gram (village) panchayaths plan-budgets in Trivandrum district, Kerala. Discussion paper series II, Centre for Development Studies.

Filmer, D., & Pritchett, L. (1998b). *Educational enrollment and attainment in India*: Household wealth, gender, village, and state effects. Mimeo. Washington, DC: World Bank. Franke, R. W., & C.

Gouda, S., & Sekher, T. V. (2014). Factors leading to school dropouts in India: An analysis of national family health survey-3 data. *IOSR Journal of Research & Method in Education*, 4(6), 75- 83.

Hashemi Syed M, Schuler Sidney Ruth, &Riley Ann P. (1996). Rural credit programs and women's empowerment in Bangladesh. World Development. 24(4): 63553.

Hatekar, N. (2009). Changing higher education scenario in India. *Economic and Political Weekly*, 44(38), 22–23.

Hazarika, Dhruba (2011). Women Empowerment in India: A Brief Discussion. *International Journal of Educational Planning & Administration*. ISSN 2249-3093 1(3) 199-202.

Hunger Project (2016) world project, http: //www. thp. org/wp

Ibrahim Solava & Alkire Sabina. (2007). Agency & Empowerment: A Proposal for Internationally Comparable Indicators. Paper prepared for the workshop 'Missing Dimensions of Poverty Data'; 2930 May. University of Oxford.

Jeffrey, C., Jeffrey, R., & Jeffrey, P. (2004). Degrees without freedom: The impact of formal education on Dalit young men in north India. Development and Change, 35(5), 963–986.

Jodhka, S. S., & Newman, K. (2007). In the name of globalisation: Meritocracy, productivity and the hidden language of caste. *Economic and Political Weekly*, 42(41), 4125–4132.

Kabeer Naila. (2001). Discussing Women's Empowerment, Theory and Practice. Sida Studies. Vol. 3. Stockholm: Swedish International Development Cooperation.

Kabeer, N. (2005). Gender equality and women's empowerment: a critical analysis of the thirdMillennium Development Goal. Gender and Development 13, no. 1: 13-24.

Kannan K. P. (1999). Poverty alleviation as advancing basic human capabilities: Kerala's achievements compared. Centre for Development Studies, Thiruvanathapuram.

Klasen S. (2006). UNDP's Gender-Related Measures: Some Conceptual Problems and Possible Solutions. *Journal of Human Development* [serial online]. 7(2): 243-274.

Klasen, Stephan & Schuler, Dana. (2011). Reforming the Gender-Related Development Index and the Gender Empowerment Measure: Implementing Some Specific Proposals. *Feminist Economics*. (1) 1 30

Kumar R. (1994). Development and Women's work in Kerala: Interactions and paradoxes. Economicand Political Weekly, 29(51-52). http: //www. thp. org/wp

Madan, A. (2020). Caste and class in higher education enrolments: challenges in conceptualizing social inequality. *Economic and Political Weekly*, 55(30), 40-47.

Malhotra, Anju Sidney Ruth Schuler, Carol Boender (2002). Measuring Women's Empowerment as a Variable in International Development Background Paper Prepared for the World Bank Workshop on Poverty and Gender: New Perspectives.

Malhotra Anju, Schuler Sidney Ruth. (2005). Women's empowerment as a variable in international development In: Narayan Deepa., editor. Measuring Empowerment: Cross-Disciplinary Perspectives. Washington, DC: World Bank.

Mamgain, Rajendra P. (2013), "Situating Scheduled Castes and Scheduled Tribes in the Post-2015 Development Framework", *Oxfam India Working Papers Series*, OIWPS-XIX, June.

Mason Karen & Smith Herbert (2003). Women's Empowerment and Social Context: Results from Five Asian Countries. Washington, DC: World Bank Gender and Development Group.

Mosedale, Sarah(2003)Assessing women's empowerment: towards a conceptual framework. Journal of International Development, 243257. Mukherjee V. N. & T. N. Seema (2000). Gender governance and citizenship in decentralized planning. Paper presented at the International conference on Democratic Decentralisation, May 23-27 Thiruvanathapuram, Kerala State Planning Board.

Naved Ruchira T. & Persson L. A. (2005). Factors associated with spousal physical violence against women in Bangladesh. Studies in Family Planning. 36: 289300.

Oommen, M. A. (2004)Deeping decentralised governance in rural India. Working paper No. 11, Centre for Socio-economic & Environmental Studies.

Panda, Pradeep Kumar (1999). Poverty and young women's employment; Linkages in Kerela. Working paper 292, Centre for Development Studies, Thiruvananthapuram.

Parveen, Shahnaj &Leonhauser- Ute, Ingrid. (2004). Empowerment of Rural Women in Bangladesh: A Household Analysis. Paper Presented in Conference on Rural Poverty Reduction through Research for Development and Transformation.

Pereznieto, Paola&Taylor, Georgia (2014). A review of approaches and methods to measure economic empowerment of women and girls. *Journal of*

Gender & Development. Volume 22 Issue 2 Gender, Monitoring, Evaluation and Learning.

Pittman, Alexandra (2014). Fast-Forwarding Gender Equality and Women's Empowerment? Reflections on Measuring Change for UNDP's Thematic Evaluation on Gender Mainstreaming and Gender Equality 2008- 2013. Independent evaluation office occasional paper.

Prahant Warke, Neelima and Parag A. Narkheda (2009). Women empowerment: skill enhancement through encouraging entrepreneurship. TactfulManagement Research Journal. ISSN 2319-7943, Impact factor 2. 1632.

Raj, R. (2013). Dalit women as political agents: A Kerala experience. *Economic and Political Weekly*, 56-63.

Rajan, R. S. (2013). Theory in the Mirror of Caste. Comparative Studies of South Asia, Africa and the Middle East, 33(3), 391-397.

Rajesh K. (2010). Reproduction of Institutions through People's Practices: Evidences from a Gram panchayath in Kerala, working paper 254. The Institute for Social and Economic Change, Bangalore.

Sabharwal, N. S. (2021). Nature of access to higher education in India: emerging pattern of social and spatial inequalities in educational opportunities. In

Reflections on 21st Century Human Habitats in India (pp. 345-369). Springer, Singapore.

Sadan, Elisheva (1997). Empowerment and Community Planning: Theory and Practice of People-Focused Social Solutions. 137-168 Tel Aviv: Hakibbutz Hameuchad Publishers.

Sahoo, Ansuman(2013) Self Help Group & Woman Empowerment: A study on some selected SHGs, International Journal of Business and Management Schuler Sidney Ruth &Hashemi Syed M. (1994). Credit programs, women's empowerment, and contraceptive use in rural Bangladesh. Studies in Family Planning. 25(2): 6576. [ ].

Saith, Ashwani, 2005, 'Poverty lines versus the Poor: Method versus Meaning', *Economic and Political Weekly*, Vol. 40 (43), October 22 – 28.

Scaria, S. (2009). Looking Beyond Literacy: Disparities in Levels of and Access to Education in a Kerala Village. Gujarat Institute of Development Research.

Scaria, S. (2014). Do caste and class define inequality? Revisiting education in a Kerala village. Contemporary Education Dialogue, 11(2), 153-177., Pushpalatha. N, 2, Dr Ramesh. B. (2020). *International Journal of Multidisciplinary and Current Educational Research* (*IJMCER*) ISSN: 2581-7027 Volume 2 Issue 5, Pages 113-119, 2020.

Scaria, S. (2014). Do caste and class define inequality? Revisiting education in a Kerala village. *Contemporary Education Dialogue*, 11(2), 153-177.

Schuler Sidney Ruth, Hashemi Syed M & Riley Ann P. (1997). The influence of changing roles and status in Bangladesh's fertility transition: evidence from a study of credit programs and contraceptive use. World Development. 25(4): 56375.

Schuler Sidney Ruth. (2007). Rural Bangladesh: sound policies, evolving gender norms and family strategies. In: Lewis EM, Lockheed M, editors. Exclusion, Gender and Education: Case Studies from the Developing World. Washington, DC: Center for Global Development.

Sen, Amartya. (1999): *'Development as Freedom'*, Oxford: Oxford University Press.

Sharma, R. N., & Sharma, R. K. (2004). *Problems of education in India*. Atlantic Publishers & Dist.

Sicilia, V. (2017). From the Inside Out: Discussing Women's Empowerment with the Women's Studies Department at the University of Calicut (Doctoral dissertation).

Sinha, G. S., & Sinha, R. C. (1967). Exploration in caste stereotypes. Social Forces, 46(1), 42-47.

Thorat, S., & Attewell, P. (2007). The legacy of social exclusion: A correspondence study of job discrimination in India. *Economic and Political Weekly*, 42(41), 4141–4145.

Tilak, J. B. G. (2005). Higher education in 'Trishanku': Hanging between state and market. *Economic and Political Weekly* 40(37), 4029–4037.

Tilak, J. B. G. (2010). Neither vision nor policy for education. *Economic and Political Weekly*, 45(13), 60–64.

Timothy Besley, Rohini Pande & Vijayendra Rao (2007), Political Economy of panchayaths in South India", *Economic and Political Weekly* Vol - XLII No. 08. PubMed

Tiwari, Nupur(2012). Women and panchayathi Raj. YOJANA, vol 56, 36-40.

UN Millennium Project. (2005). Taking Action: Achieving Gender Equality and Empowering Women. Task Force on Education and Gender Equality. London: Earthscan.

UNDP. (1995). Human Development Report: The World's Women 1995: Trends and Statistics. New York, NY: Oxford University Press and UNDP; 1995.

United Nations. (1996). The Beijing Declaration and Platform for Action. New York, NY: United Nations.

University Grants Commission. (2008). Higher education in India. Issues related to expansion, inclusiveness, quality, and finance.

University Grants Commission. (2008). Higher education in India. Issues related to expansion, inclusiveness, quality and finance.

Williams, Jill(2005). Gender and Women's Empowerment Using Confirmatory Factor Analysis, Research Program on Population Processes. Population Aging Centre, University of Colorado.

Yamuna et. al (2013) panchayath Raj Institutions as an Instrument for Women Empowerment-A Case Study, *IOSR Journal Of Humanities And Social Science (IOSRJHSS)*, 8(4) 06-09

Zachariah K. C., Irudaya Rajan S., Sarma P. S, Navaneetham K., Gopinathan Nair P. S. & Mishra U. S. (1994). Demographic transition in Kerala in the 1980s. Centre for Development Studies-Monograph series. Thiruvananthapuram, Tilak baker, CDS

Abdul Salim, A., & Gopinathan Nair, P. R. (2002). *Educational development in India*: The Kerala experience since 1800. New Delhi: Anmol.

Alkire, Sabina (2007). Measuring Agency: Issues and Possibilities. *Indian Journal of Human Development*. Vol. 1(1).

Anand Jaya S. (2002). Self-Help Groups in Empowering Women: Case study of selected SHGs and NHGs, Discussion Paper No. 38. Kerala Research Programme on Local Level Development.

Arya, S., & Rathore, A. S. (Eds.). (2019). Dalit feminist theory: A reader. Taylor & Francis.

Asrani, S., & Kaushik, S. (2011). *Problems perceived by scheduled caste women in Haryana.* Studies of Tribes and Tribals, 9(1), 29-36.

Basu, Ramit (2010). The Role of the Gram Sabha in the process of planning - An analytical approach, Proceedings of the National Seminar on Grama sabha edited by S. A. Ashraful Hasan and G. S. Ganesh Prasad, Abdul Nazir Sab State Institute of Rural Development, Mysore Government of Karnataka

Bates Lisa M., Schuler Sidney Ruth & Islam Farzana. (2004). Socioeconomic factors and processes associated with domestic violence in rural Bangladesh. International Family Planning Perspectives. 30: 190-199.

Beecher, Catharine Esther & Beecher Stove Harriet (1869). *The American Women's Home*. NewYork, J. B. Ford Company.

Beteta Cueva, Hanny (2006). What is missing in measures of women's empowerment? *Journal of Human Development*. 7(2): 22141.

Bhagavatheeswaran, L., Nair, S., Stone, H., Isac, S., Hiremath, T., Raghavendra, T., ... & Beattie, T. S. (2016). The barriers and enablers to education among scheduled caste and scheduled tribe adolescent girls in northern Karnataka, South India: A qualitative study. *International journal of educational development,* 49, 262-270.

Biswas (1999). Measuring Women's empowerment some methodological issues. *Asia-Pacific Journal of Rural Development* Vol. 9, No. 2, P. 63-71.

Borah, Ajit (2014). Women empowerment through Self Help Groups-A case study of Barhampur Development Block in Nagaon District of Assam. *IOSR Journal of Economics and Finance* (IOSR-JEF) e-ISSN: 2321- 5933, p-ISSN: 2321-5925. 4 (3) 56-62.

Bui Chung, Daisy Kulvatee Kantachote, Asmah Mallick, Rachel Polster, Kelsey Roets (2013). Indicators of Women's Empowerment in Developing Nations, Paper presented in the Workshop in International Public Affairs, Robert M. La Follette School of Public Affairs.

Census 2011. Ministry of Statistics, Government of India.

Chanana, K. (1993). Accessing higher education: the dilemma of schooling women, minorities, Scheduled Castes and Scheduled Tribes in contemporary India. Higher Education, 26(1), 69-92.

Charmes J & Wieringa S. (2003). Measuring Women's Empowerment: An Assessment of the GenderRelated Development Index and the Gender

Empowerment Measure. *Journal of Human Development* [serial online, 4(3): 419-435.

Chetia, Madhurya & Devajyoti Gogoi (2013), Empowerment of women through panchayathi raj system, *International Journal of Humanities and Social Science Invention* ISSN, 2(6), 05-09.

Das, Suchitra (2014). Women Participation in panchayathi Raj: A Case Study of Karimganj District of Assam, *International Journal of Humanities & Social Science Studies* (IJHSSS), Volume-I, Issue-I, pp 52- 58.

Deshpande, A., & Newman, K. (2007). Where the path leads: The role of caste in post-university employment expectations. *Economic and Political Weekly*, 42(41), 4133–4140.

Deshpande, S. (2006). Exclusive inequalities: Merit, caste and discrimination in Indian higher education today. *Economic and Political Weekly*, 41(24), 2438–2444.

Devaki, Jane (1990). Development, Theory and Practice, Insights Emer ging fr om Women's Experience. *Economic and Political Weekly*, 22(27), 1454-55.

Devi Lakshmy, K. R. (1996). Determinants of Labour Force Participation among Women in Kerala- Some Evidence from a Micro Level Study. *The Asian Economic Review*, 38(4).

Devi, Lakshmy, K. R. (2002). Education, Employment and Job preference of woman in Kerala: A micro level case study. Discussion paper No: 42, *Kerala Research Programme on Local level Development*, CDS, Trivandrum.

Dunn, D. (1993). Gender inequality in education and employment in the scheduled castes and tribes of India. *Population Research and Policy Review*, 12(1), 53-70.

Eapen, Mridual & Thomas, Soya (2005). Gender analysis of select gram (village) panchayaths plan-budgets in Trivandrum district, Kerala. Discussion paper series II, Centre for Development Studies.

Filmer, D., & Pritchett, L. (1998b). *Educational enrollment and attainment in India*: Household wealth, gender, village, and state effects. Mimeo. Washington, DC: World Bank. Franke, R. W., & C.

Gouda, S., & Sekher, T. V. (2014). Factors leading to school dropouts in India: An analysis of national family health survey-3 data. *IOSR Journal of Research & Method in Education*, 4(6), 75- 83.

Hashemi Syed M, Schuler Sidney Ruth, &Riley Ann P. (1996). Rural credit programs and women's empowerment in Bangladesh. World Development. 24(4): 63553.

Hatekar, N. (2009). Changing higher education scenario in India. *Economic and Political Weekly*, 44(38), 22–23.

Hazarika, Dhruba (2011). Women Empowerment in India: A Brief Discussion. *International Journal of Educational Planning & Administration*. ISSN 2249-3093 1(3) 199-202.

Hunger Project (2016) world project, http: //www. thp. org/wp

Ibrahim Solava & Alkire Sabina. (2007). Agency & Empowerment: A Proposal for Internationally Comparable Indicators. Paper prepared for the workshop 'Missing Dimensions of Poverty Data'; 2930 May. University of Oxford.

Jeffrey, C., Jeffrey, R., & Jeffrey, P. (2004). Degrees without freedom: The impact of formal education on Dalit young men in north India. Development and Change, 35(5), 963–986.

Jodhka, S. S., & Newman, K. (2007). In the name of globalisation: Meritocracy, productivity and the hidden language of caste. *Economic and Political Weekly*, 42(41), 4125–4132.

Kabeer Naila. (2001). Discussing Women's Empowerment, Theory and Practice. Sida Studies. Vol. 3. Stockholm: Swedish International Development Cooperation.

Kabeer, N. (2005). Gender equality and women's empowerment: a critical analysis of the thirdMillennium Development Goal. Gender and Development 13, no. 1: 13-24.

Kannan K. P. (1999). Poverty alleviation as advancing basic human capabilities: Kerala's achievements compared. Centre for Development Studies, Thiruvanathapuram.

Klasen S. (2006). UNDP's Gender-Related Measures: Some Conceptual Problems and Possible Solutions. *Journal of Human Development* [serial online]. 7(2): 243-274.

Klasen, Stephan & Schuler, Dana. (2011). Reforming the Gender-Related Development Index and the Gender Empowerment Measure: Implementing Some Specific Proposals. *Feminist Economics*. (1) 1 30

Kumar R. (1994). Development and Women's work in Kerala: Interactions and paradoxes. Economicand Political Weekly, 29(51-52). http: //www. thp. org/wp

Madan, A. (2020). Caste and class in higher education enrolments: challenges in conceptualizing social inequality. *Economic and Political Weekly*, 55(30), 40-47.

Malhotra, Anju Sidney Ruth Schuler, Carol Boender (2002). Measuring Women's Empowerment as a Variable in International Development Background

Paper Prepared for the World Bank Workshop on Poverty and Gender: New Perspectives.

Malhotra Anju, Schuler Sidney Ruth. (2005). Women's empowerment as a variable in international development In: Narayan Deepa., editor. Measuring Empowerment: Cross-Disciplinary Perspectives. Washington, DC: World Bank.

Mamgain, Rajendra P. (2013), "Situating Scheduled Castes and Scheduled Tribes in the Post-2015 Development Framework", *Oxfam India Working Papers Series*, OIWPS-XIX, June.

Mason Karen & Smith Herbert (2003). Women's Empowerment and Social Context: Results from Five Asian Countries. Washington, DC: World Bank Gender and Development Group.

Mosedale, Sarah(2003)Assessing women's empowerment: towards a conceptual framework. Journal of International Development, 243257. Mukherjee V. N. & T. N. Seema (2000). Gender governance and citizenship in decentralized planning. Paper presented at the International conference on Democratic Decentralisation, May 23-27 Thiruvanathapuram, Kerala State Planning Board.

Naved Ruchira T. & Persson L. A. (2005). Factors associated with spousal physical violence against women in Bangladesh. Studies in Family Planning. 36: 289300.

Oommen, M. A. (2004)Deeping decentralised governance in rural India. Working paper No. 11, Centre for Socio-economic & Environmental Studies.

Panda, Pradeep Kumar (1999). Poverty and young women's employment; Linkages in Kerela. Working paper 292, Centre for Development Studies, Thiruvananthapuram.

Parveen, Shahnaj &Leonhauser- Ute, Ingrid. (2004). Empowerment of Rural Women in Bangladesh: A Household Analysis. Paper Presented in Conference on Rural Poverty Reduction through Research for Development and Transformation.

Pereznieto, Paola&Taylor, Georgia (2014). A review of approaches and methods to measure economic empowerment of women and girls. *Journal of Gender & Development*. Volume 22 Issue 2 Gender, Monitoring, Evaluation and Learning.

Pittman, Alexandra (2014). Fast-Forwarding Gender Equality and Women's Empowerment? Reflections on Measuring Change for UNDP's Thematic Evaluation on Gender Mainstreaming and Gender Equality 2008- 2013. Independent evaluation office occasional paper.

Prahant Warke, Neelima and Parag A. Narkheda (2009). Women empowerment: skill enhancement through encouraging entrepreneurship. TactfulManagement Research Journal. ISSN 2319-7943, Impact factor 2. 1632.

Raj, R. (2013). Dalit women as political agents: A Kerala experience. *Economic and Political Weekly*, 56-63.

Rajan, R. S. (2013). Theory in the Mirror of Caste. Comparative Studies of South Asia, Africa and the Middle East, 33(3), 391-397.

Rajesh K. (2010). Reproduction of Institutions through People's Practices: Evidences from a Gram panchayath in Kerala, working paper 254. The Institute for Social and Economic Change, Bangalore.

Sabharwal, N. S. (2021). Nature of access to higher education in India: emerging pattern of social and spatial inequalities in educational opportunities. In Reflections on 21st Century Human Habitats in India (pp. 345-369). Springer, Singapore.

Sadan, Elisheva (1997). Empowerment and Community Planning: Theory and Practice of People-Focused Social Solutions. 137-168 Tel Aviv: Hakibbutz Hameuchad Publishers.

Sahoo, Ansuman(2013) Self Help Group & Woman Empowerment: A study on some selected SHGs, International Journal of Business and Management

Schuler Sidney Ruth &Hashemi Syed M. (1994). Credit programs, women's empowerment, and contraceptive use in rural Bangladesh. Studies in Family Planning. 25(2): 6576. [ ].

Saith, Ashwani, 2005, 'Poverty lines versus the Poor: Method versus Meaning', *Economic and Political Weekly*, Vol. 40 (43), October 22 – 28.

Scaria, S. (2009). Looking Beyond Literacy: Disparities in Levels of and Access to Education in a Kerala Village. Gujarat Institute of Development Research.

Scaria, S. (2014). Do caste and class define inequality? Revisiting education in a Kerala village. Contemporary Education Dialogue, 11(2), 153-177., Pushpalatha. N, 2, Dr Ramesh. B. (2020). *International Journal of Multidisciplinary and Current Educational Research* (*IJMCER*) ISSN: 2581-7027 Volume 2 Issue 5, Pages 113-119, 2020.

Scaria, S. (2014). Do caste and class define inequality? Revisiting education in a Kerala village. *Contemporary Education Dialogue*, 11(2), 153-177.

Schuler Sidney Ruth, Hashemi Syed M & Riley Ann P. (1997). The influence of changing roles and status in Bangladesh's fertility transition: evidence from a study of credit programs and contraceptive use. World Development. 25(4): 56375.

Schuler Sidney Ruth. (2007). Rural Bangladesh: sound policies, evolving gender norms and family strategies. In: Lewis EM, Lockheed M, editors. Exclusion, Gender and Education: Case Studies from the Developing World. Washington, DC: Center for Global Development.

Sen, Amartya. (1999): *'Development as Freedom'*, Oxford: Oxford University Press.

Sharma, R. N., & Sharma, R. K. (2004). *Problems of education in India*. Atlantic Publishers & Dist.

Sicilia, V. (2017). From the Inside Out: Discussing Women's Empowerment with the Women's Studies Department at the University of Calicut (Doctoral dissertation).

Sinha, G. S., & Sinha, R. C. (1967). Exploration in caste stereotypes. Social Forces, 46(1), 42-47.

Thorat, S., & Attewell, P. (2007). The legacy of social exclusion: A correspondence study of job discrimination in India. *Economic and Political Weekly*, 42(41), 4141–4145.

Tilak, J. B. G. (2005). Higher education in 'Trishanku': Hanging between state and market. *Economic and Political Weekly* 40(37), 4029–4037.

Tilak, J. B. G. (2010). Neither vision nor policy for education. *Economic and Political Weekly*, 45(13), 60–64.

Timothy Besley, Rohini Pande & Vijayendra Rao (2007), Political Economy of panchayaths in South India", *Economic and Political Weekly* Vol - XLII No. 08. PubMed

Tiwari, Nupur(2012). Women and panchayathi Raj. YOJANA, vol 56, 36-40.

UN Millennium Project. (2005). Taking Action: Achieving Gender Equality and Empowering Women. Task Force on Education and Gender Equality. London: Earthscan.

UNDP. (1995). Human Development Report: The World's Women 1995: Trends and Statistics. New York, NY: Oxford University Press and UNDP; 1995.

United Nations. (1996). The Beijing Declaration and Platform for Action. New York, NY: United Nations.

University Grants Commission. (2008). Higher education in India. Issues related to expansion, inclusiveness, quality, and finance.

University Grants Commission. (2008). Higher education in India. Issues related to expansion, inclusiveness, quality and finance.

Williams, Jill(2005). Gender and Women's Empowerment Using Confirmatory Factor Analysis, Research Program on Population Processes. Population Aging Centre, University of Colorado.

Yamuna et. al (2013) panchayath Raj Institutions as an Instrument for Women Empowerment-A Case Study, *IOSR Journal Of Humanities And Social Science (IOSRJHSS)*, 8(4) 06-09

Zachariah K. C., Irudaya Rajan S., Sarma P. S, Navaneetham K., Gopinathan Nair P. S. & Mishra U. S. (1994). Demographic transition in Kerala in the 1980s. Centre for Development Studies-Monograph series. Thiruvananthapuram, Tilak baker, CDS

Biography

Aysha shameer, She is not just a women made a path of number of women. Aysha a native of palakkad carriers legacy of her parents Rukkiya and Rafeeq. she was born on 10th August 1993. She completed her primary education at pathripala from Mount Seena school. As her father expired at her young age. After that she studied in Ansar school perumpilavu Trissur, she was then married off. That didn't stop her. After marriage and having kids completed her plus two education,She earned her Bachelor's Degree and Masters in English literature From Bharathiar University with the great support of her husband shameer k, and after that she has successfully completed her second pg in Women's Studies from Calicut University campus, demonstrating her dedication to understanding and advocating for gender equality through an in-depth exploration of gender theory, and the historical context of women's movements. This academic achievement underscores her commitment to making meaningful contributions in fields such as social justice, human rights, and public policy. She initiated a library in her home where children and women from nearby locality rely upon.In the library more than five thousand books, through library doing various social services like conducting Awareness programs, and supporting neighbourhood children for their education. She is also Women Activist too. who helps in upbringing women forward and help them to realise their actual potential. She is a good teacher who teaches from heart also completed TTC, she had list of pen friends, She got reply from newzealand former prime minister Jacinda Ardern with her signature. a popular incident in her life and also she received women Substance Network Award from Hypgge media Rajasthan.

www.ingramcontent.com/pod-product-compliance
Lightning Source LLC
LaVergne TN
LVHW021140160826
845679LV00023B/1982